P9-DEC-586

Angels Over
Their Shoulders

Angels Over Their Shoulders

Children's Encounters with Heavenly Beings

BRAD STEIGER
SHERRY HANSEN STEIGER

Guideposts®

CARMEL • NEW YORK 10512

This Guideposts edition is published by special arrangement with
Fawcett Columbine/Ballantine Books.

http:/www.guideposts.org

Copyright © 1995 by Brad Steiger and Sherry Hansen Steiger

All rights reserved under International and Pan-American Copyright Conventions.

Library of Congress Catalog Card Number: 94-94579

ISBN: 0-449-90963-8

Cover and book design by José R. Fonfrias
Typeset by Composition Technologies, Inc.
Manufactured in the United States of America

Contents

Angels Over Their Shoulders

 VERY OLD TRADITION SAYS that guardian angels are appointed to children at the time of their birth, and our research into contemporary accounts of these multidimensional beings verifies that angels do have a special interest in protecting children, almost as if they were ethereal surrogate parents.

The seventeenth-century mystic Amos Komensky declared that each child has an angel, "given to him by God and ordained to be his guardian, that [the angel] might guard him, preserve him, and protect him against all dangers and snares, pits, ambushes, traps, and temptations."

In *Angels Over Their Shoulders: Children's Encounters with Heavenly Beings,* we recount dozens of inspirational stories in which children interacted with angels— miraculous accounts in which angels have rescued children from burning buildings, brought them blankets when they were freezing, water when they were dehydrating, baby formula when they were dying for the need of proper nourishment. We share dramatic, inspirational reports of angelic healing ministers, heavenly messengers, and deathbed comforters.

And we also recount the moving narratives of those children who had their lives transformed through the catalyst of a personal blending with angelic intelligence.

Beautiful Beings of Light

When seen on earth accomplishing their various missions, angels are consistently said to appear youthful, commanding, beautiful of countenance, and often majestic and awesome. Manifestations of light often accompany them, which lend to the grandeur of their general appearance and the feelings of profound reverence that suffuse those who encounter angelic beings.

Yet not all angels appear as blond, blue-eyed entities in flowing white robes. Angels have the ability to appear in a variety of forms and with a wide range of physical characteristics. And not all angels have human forms and characteristics. They seem completely capable of shaping reality in our three-dimensional world to suit their heavenly purposes. In certain cases, they may even reveal themselves as beings of pure light.

And while the majority of instances described in this book deal with a single dramatic angelic interaction that changed—or preserved—a child's life, we shall also meet a number of individuals who have been able to enjoy a lifelong relationship with guardian angels they first met as children.

Citizens from an Unseen World

People have always believed in unseen intelligences inhabiting an invisible realm in proximity to our own world. The holy books of nearly all religious belief structures support such ideas, and tell their followers that such spiritual entities as angels do most certainly exist.

In nearly all stories of angels, the beings are paraphysical—that is, they are both material and nonmaterial entities. Although they would appear to originate in some invisible and nonphysical dimension, they are often seen to manifest as solidly in our reality as those humans whose lives they seek to affect.

There is no question that in both the Old and New Testaments angels are considered fully capable of becoming quite physical and material—at least long enough to accomplish their appointed mission of rescue, healing, or guidance. Throughout the Bible we read of angels who wrestled with stubborn shepherds, guided people lost in the wilderness, and freed persecuted prophets from fiery furnaces and dank prisons. Jesus himself was fed by angels, defended by angels, and strengthened by angels.

Although angels are frequently described as being strong, swift, and majestic, the awesome beings themselves very often caution those with whom they interact that they are not to be held as objects of veneration or worship.

Dr. Billy Graham, the popular clergyman, stressed a similar point in his best-selling book *Angels: God's Secret Agents:* "Angels are indeed mightier than men, but they are not gods and they do not possess the attributes of the Godhead."

Numerous passages in the Bible indicate that angels have additional boundaries. Their physical powers are limited, as is their knowledge—although their active interest in the affairs of humans remains always their principal concern. According to tradition, angels stand ever ready to guide, help, and defend us against the trials and temptations of life on Earth.

BELIEF IN ANGELS REMAINS STRONG—AND IT'S GROWING!

Recent research has produced all kinds of evidence that large numbers of people believe very strongly in angels and take great comfort from the knowledge of their existence.

In a March 1993 Gallup survey, statistics indicated that teenagers in the United States were more likely to believe in angels than at any time in the past fifteen years. According to the poll, seventy-six percent of the teens said that they believed in the existence of angels, a percentage that the pollsters noted has been steadily increasing since a survey conducted in 1978, when only sixty-four percent admitted to a belief in angels.

THE STEIGER TWENTY-FIVE-YEAR SURVEY OF MYSTICAL AND ANGELIC EXPERIENCES

As children, we also experienced interaction with entities that we believed to be angels; and as adults, we are convinced that we were brought together as man and wife through the remarkable intervention of an angel who temporarily took control of a complete stranger to make the crucial introductions.

Over a period of twenty-five years, we have been providing a questionnaire to readers of our books and attendees of our seminars and lectures who claim to have experienced some form of contact with an otherworldly being. Of the more than twenty thousand respondents who have thus far answered our questionnaire, a remarkable ninety percent tell of having received a visitation from an angelic or multidimensional being as early as the age of five; and over fifty percent believe that the same entity they encountered as children continues to serve as their guardian or guide through the hazardous course of life.

Here are some of their inspirational stories:

ANGELIC RESCUERS

An Angel Kept the Two Girls Afloat in the River Until Human Help Came

Dr. L. Larson, a retired clergyman from Moorhead, Minnesota, spoke of the time when two sisters, aged eight and four, fell into a river near the church where he had his parish ministry.

While the hysterical mother screamed that her daughters could not swim, a man who had been fishing from a boat set out at once on a rescue attempt. Although the fisherman was determined to make a valiant effort, in his heart he felt that there would be no way that he could reach the little girls before they drowned. He truly feared that his efforts would be futile.

When he pulled alongside them, however, he found the little girls floating calmly in an "unnatural manner," as if they were "somehow supported from underneath."

Dr. Larson said that men and women who had watched the rescue from the shore stated that they had seen a beautiful person in white supporting the girls until the fisherman overtook them. The girls themselves insisted that an angel had prevented them from sinking under the water, and they described their ethereal rescuer in vivid detail.

She Was Warned
to Escape a Bolt of Lightning

Ann is a bank teller from Grand Rapids, Michigan, who remembers that at age eight a voice awakened her during a thunderstorm and told her to get out of bed at once. If she had not obeyed, she notes wryly, she would not have been writing to us today "because seconds later lightning hit the metal screen above my bed and shot across my pillow."

A Mother's Premonition of Death
Is Averted by Her Son's Guardian Angel

Alice Charles of Arlington Heights, Illinois, told us of the time when she had a terrible premonition that her four-year-old son, Samuel, had been struck and killed by a swiftly moving truck.

When she ran to the scene where she had envisioned the horrible accident, she found Samuel unharmed. However, *both* the child and witnesses to the near tragedy stated that a figure in white, emanating a brilliant light, had appeared at the last possible moment to snatch Samuel from certain death under the wheels of a speeding truck.

Rescued by an Angel
from a Fall Through the Ice

Linda Jo is an emergency medical technician in Columbiaville, Michigan. She was about eight years old when she was lying in bed, crying out all her unhappiness.

"I felt a presence in the room and, turning, I saw a beautiful woman whose shape was all in shining white. She was standing by my bed, smiling at me. She did not speak, but she reached down and stroked my hair. The love and the warmth from her caused me to relax and to drift off to sleep."

When Linda Jo was nineteen, she fell through the ice of a lake on a cold day in February. She was alone, and no one could hear her screams for help. The cold water was about to pull her under.

"And then a voice came to me and began giving me instructions on how to get out of the water. I obeyed the instructions and, as exhausted as I was, I managed to get out.

"To this day I am warned of danger by my angel. Usually the warnings come in the form of a voice inside my head."

Snatched from Beneath
the Wheels of a Speeding Truck

Phyllis of Cedar Falls, Iowa, still maintains contact with the robed angelic mentor who saved her life when she was five years old:

"Mother called for me to return home, and I ran out into the street, not noticing the traffic. Too late I saw the oncoming truck and, trying to stop, I fell into its path. My angel in his white robe pulled me away just in time. He told me that it was not my time yet."

ANGELIC HEALINGS

Angelic beings are often the ministers of miraculous healings for children.

Mrs. David Mcnight of Lincoln, Nebraska, remembered the time that her fourteen-year-old daughter, Cindy, was in a nearby park caring for Billy, the five-year-old asthmatic son of a neighbor.

According to Cindy and the boy, a blue-eyed, golden-haired angel appeared beside them, then knelt and kissed Billy. Almost at once the child's difficulty with his breathing ceased, and Billy was never again troubled by severe respiratory problems. Cindy later told her mother how the angel had manifested in answer to her prayers for divine healing for young Billy.

The Angel's Healing Kiss
Made Rebekah "All Better" for Christmas

Raymond Blomker and his wife had been told by several doctors that their seven-year-old daughter, Rebekah, would not recover from her lengthy illness. Each time the child began to speak of Christmas and the gifts that she most wanted, Blomker's heart felt as if it were being wrenched from his chest.

One night in October, as Blomker and his wife were praying for a miracle of healing at their sleeping daughter's bedside, they were distracted by the sound of a soft tapping on the windowpane.

To their astonishment, they saw a glowing light—which further startled them by moving through the closed window and materializing into an angel within Rebekah's bedroom. The being walked over to the sleeping child, bent to place a gentle kiss on her cheek, then disappeared.

Within moments Rebekah opened her eyes sleepily and smiled. "Can I get up and play now?" she asked, stifling a yawn. "My angel was just here and made me all better."

The next day the doctors confirmed for the Blomkers that they had received their miracle. Rebekah would live to see that Christmas and many, many more.

A Beautiful Lady Clothed
in Purple Came to Comfort Her

Elsie Tyler from Anderson, Indiana, recalls her experience with a solicitious angel when she was a child of five.

"I was in the hospital to have my tonsils and adenoids removed," she said. "Sadly for me, my mother was in the same hospital at the same time, awaiting the birth of my brother."

Little Elsie wanted her mother near her during the surgery, and she remembered fighting the ether cone and throwing it across the room a couple of times, before the nurses and orderlies held her down.

"I awoke alone in a crib and in awful pain," she said. "It hurt to cry, but it hurt more to be alone, without my mother."

Suddenly, from out of nowhere, a beautiful lady clothed in purple appeared beside her crib and began to comfort her. "She told me that everything would be okay. She said that my mother was in a room upstairs and that she was all right."

Words of reassurance were inadequate to soothe a five-year-old who had just had her tonsils removed, and Elsie began once again to cry that she wanted to see her mother.

"The lady in purple stood quietly for a moment, as if she were thinking things over," Elsie said. "Then she bent down and picked me up. I knew that she was going to take me to my mother.

"Just then we could hear someone coming down the hall. The lady in purple quickly placed me back in the crib, then disappeared.

"A few moments later a nurse walked into the room. 'Do you know that you've just had a baby brother, Elsie?' she asked with a broad smile.

"When I asked the nurse if I could see my mother, she shook her head and started to deny my request—but then she suddenly shrugged and said, 'I don't see any reason why I can't carry you up for a quick peek at your mommy.'

"I know that the lady in purple was my guardian angel and that she telepathically changed the nurse's mind," Elsie Tyler concluded. "Later I told Mom about the lady, but I don't know if she ever believed me."

THE MARVELOUS APPEARANCES OF ANGELS

Reverend W. Bennett Palmer, a retired Protestant clergyman, contacted us in the early 1970s with the results of his extensive study about the manner in which angels appear and disappear to and from the lives of those—young and old, children and adults—whom they so dramatically touch. The collection of first-person accounts of angelic encounters became the late Reverend Palmer's avocation, and he spent decades meticulously and respectfully interviewing hundreds of witnesses of angelic manifestations. The following material is adapted from Reverend Palmer's notes and is presented as a memorial to his great labor of love and devotion.

Here is how angels have appeared to observers:

- The heavens appear to open, and an angel is seen to descend directly into the presence of the human observer
- A shaft of light is first seen emanating from the sky as a kind of signal to the witness; when the heavenly illumination has been perceived, the angel comes toward the person receiving the vision
- A tunnel may appear to open up in the physical environment, and the angel emerges to approach the person having the vision
- The angel may at first be seen at some distance, and then is observed by the percipient to walk into his or her presence

- A very commonly reported angelic manifestation occurs when the angel appears to come through the wall of a room or through a closed door. The angel may also leave in the same manner
- In other accounts, the angel is said to open a door and to walk into a room where the human observer is at the time
- The human testifier may hear footsteps outside the house and hear a knock at the door. When he or she opens the door, the angel is revealed
- The angel may materialize in one part of a room, then walk toward the witness and converse with him or her
- Frequently, the face of an angel may appear as if it were a picture on the wall
- Angels are often seen in churches, walking down aisles or standing in some particular part of the building
- In many cases, the beneficiary of the visitation is awakened from sleep by an angel, and the holy figure is seen standing near or bending over the recipient
- The recipient of the vision or visitation, while in bed but still awake, feels a strong presence in the room and then sees the angel materialize
- The percipient hears a voice telling him or her to "look up." When the percipient complies, the image of an angel is seen
- A cloud is seen moving toward the recipient of the experience. As it draws near, an angel emerges from within. Conversely, there are accounts of angels disappearing into a cloud
- In some accounts, a cloud or a mist appears within a room, then permits an angel to emerge from its midst
- The testifier is awakened by the shining of a bright light in the room. When he or she sits up, an angel is seen
- The recipient of the experience is engaged in conversation with a total

stranger, who proceeds to relate his or her innermost thoughts and concerns. At the termination of the dialogue, the stranger reveals himself to be an angel

- The percipient may have a vision of numerous angels forming an aisle to permit one central angel to approach
- Many visions of angels occur in connection with statues of the heavenly messengers, and the percipient observes the images come to life
- There are some interesting accounts in which an angel appears in a room in which one person is awake and the other is asleep—yet both are able to "see" the same manifestation. The recipient who is awake sees the angel as an objective manifestation, while the sleeper perceives the angelic being in a dream
- Numerous accounts tell of an angel who manifests to several persons at the same time, yet is perceived differently by various individuals in the group. For one individual, the angel may have appeared as a flash of light; for another, as a luminous ball or cloud; for yet another as an apparition in human form; and for still others as a presence only, perceived by an inner or outer voice
- An angel may also manifest to many persons in a group and be seen as a solid being by all of them, some of them, or by only one of them
- Angels appear frequently in dreams that are indistinguishable from ordinary dreams—except that they very often produce miraculous healings
- Angels often are reported to manifest as supernatural allies when the recipient of the visitation feels that he or she is struggling against evil
- Many recipients who have recovered from serious illnesses have stated that they saw angels standing at the foot of their bed
- Angels may instantly disappear after they have interacted with a testifier, or they may gradually fade away. In some instances angels are seen to walk away and to disappear into the distance. Angels have been observed passing through walls,

closed doors, or ascending through ceilings. On occasion, angels take leave of the recipient by walking out the door in a natural human manner

- A very impressive kind of visitation has the angel emerging from a bright supernatural light, which illuminates the entire room or area of materialization
- In other accounts of similar visitations, no angel manifests from within the supernatural light, but a voice, an influence, or a healing emanates from the bright globe of illumination
- Many people have told of encountering an angel while undergoing an out-of-body experience. The recipient may see his or her physical body lying in bed—and while thus out of the body perceives the angel, which had previously been invisible
- In other accounts of out-of-body experience, the percipient claims to have traveled to distant homes or to hospital rooms of friends and loved ones and to have seen an angel at the bedside of the afflicted one
- As might be anticipated, contemporary technology has been involved in many reports of angels. Supernatural voices have been heard over the telephone, and many have been impressed on tape recorders. Angels have been photographed, and their images have been captured by motion picture and video cameras. Percipients have increasingly reported observing the face of an angel on the television screen while viewing a telecast

An Overflowing of Angelic Love
from the "True Reality"

Rachael Morgon of Portland, Oregon, had her first visitation of angels when she was sixteen. She was awakened in the middle of the night and saw three beings who, at that time, she "took to be Jesus and two angels."

At first she thought she might be having a dream, but then she clearly remembered waking up *before* the beings materialized in her bedroom.

The male entity communicated mentally to Rachael that she had a mission to accomplish. "I don't consciously remember what he said the mission was, but I felt so much love emanating from the beings that it was almost unbearable. Then I went back to sleep."

When she was thirty years old, Rachael was hospitalized for pneumonia, and while there in the hospital under medical supervision she fell into a coma that lasted for twenty-one days. During that time she was aware only of her angelic mentors visiting her and taking her to a place that she knew was the "true reality," a place far more beautiful and real than Earth.

His Guardian Angel Helped Him
to Endure an Abusive Childhood

Jim Halloran, a thirty-four-year-old high school teacher from Madison, Wisconsin, has always felt that the entity that first appeared to him when he was five was a guardian angel who manifested to help him through a childhood that was marred by terrible physical and mental abuse.

Jim, the youngest of four boys, was the family scapegoat, different from his three brothers in so many ways. "I have an I.Q. that is far above average, where they are exceedingly average and mentally lazy. From an early age I was very athletic, whereas they were clumsy and uncoordinated. I rarely became ill as a child, but it seemed they continually passed their various sicknesses back and forth to one another. To this day I remain the only member of my family who has never been chemically dependent."

When he was a small child, Jim not only had to survive a regular round of beatings from his older brothers, but his alcoholic parents were also well satisfied that their youngest child should serve as the whipping boy for all wrongs, real and imagined, they deemed society had dealt them.

"During these early years of dreadful abuse, my guardian angel would speak with me," Halloran told us. "He would tell me that I was worthwhile, that I was loved by God, and that I had talents and abilities that my family would never be capable of understanding.

"I never went to Sunday school or church as a child," Halloran said, "so no one could ever say in my case that I was projecting my hopes and my religious faith into a kind of imaginary friend. I didn't know what angels were until I was quite a bit older and happened to read references to the heavenly beings in various books. When I was about sixteen, I began to attend church with a friend, and today I consider myself quite religious and active in the Methodist church."

Jim Halloran is convinced that he was able to mature into a balanced young man as a result of the communication and love he received from his guardian angel.

"Knowing that my angel was always there for me enabled me to go through high school with a great deal of confidence and self-awareness. I was a straight A student in both high school and college. I worked three part-time jobs and put myself through college. I received my degree in education, and after five years of teaching, married a fellow teacher. We have two daughters on whom I shower affection—and I tell them about the eternal goodness of God and the love of their guardian angels that will always surround them."

A Lifetime of Angelic Intervention

Diana Osornio, a fifty-year-old former professor of psychology who is now a technical writer who has prepared policy and procedure manuals for a number of Fortune 500 firms, first met her guardian angel when she was five and her family was vacationing in the woods of northern Minnesota.

"I was shown bits and pieces of my future life," she told us. "My angel told me that I had a distinct purpose in life and a particular mission to accomplish. Of course, much of what he said went over my head at the time. Throughout my life I have continually flashed back to that initial visitation and remembered more of what the angel told me. For many years after my first angelic encounter, I compulsively drew pictures of heavenly beings and holy figures."

When she was eleven, Diana nearly drowned. "It was at a lake where my grandparents had their summer cottage. I was horsing around with some other kids on a floating wooden dock, and I got pushed under and trapped under the planking. All the air was squeezed out of me, and I passed out."

According to the other children on the floating dock, "a guy who kind of looked like a hippie, with long blond hair" pulled Diana out from under the planking and hauled her to the surface.

"My grandparents looked in every cabin around the lake so they could thank the fellow for saving me, but they never found anyone who fit the description that the other kids had given of my rescuer," Diana said. "I know that it was my guardian angel who pulled me to the surface and saved my life."

Diana went on to tell us that she has experienced the benefit of warning voices all her life.

"Sometimes they warn me of danger, such as a possible traffic accident around the bend. Once a voice told me to go out and buy a bunch of herbs I would never think of using and to take them in a particular sequence. Research after the fact provided verification that this formula was what I needed at the time for a major detoxification of my physical body."

Diana herself has never seen the angelic entities who have so vigilantly guided her life "except as energy forms of brilliant light."

Diana added that sometimes she wished that she were able to see the angels as others saw them. "But I believe in their existence anyway. Perhaps it is as Jesus said: 'Blessed are they that have not seen, and yet have believed.'"

THE VOLUMINOUS MAIL we have received from our readers and from those who have attended our lectures and seminars has demonstrated unequivocally that thousands of contemporary men and women are unashamedly interacting with their guardian angels, and that this contact was initiated by the angelic entities when our correspondents were very young children. What is more, these men and women come from every conceivable avenue of life. They are scientists, educators, medical doctors, nurses, psychiatrists, military officers, concert pianists, members of the clergy, law enforcement personnel, members of the armed services, social workers, journalists, entertainment figures, housewives, students, truck drivers, cowboys, farmers, and commercial fishermen—all of whom testify that they have profited materially and spiritually from contact with angelic beings who constitute a source of strength and guidance external to themselves. Join us, then, as we explore the world of children and angels.

Dramatic Rescues of Children by Angelic Beings

OR CENTURIES, MEN AND WOMEN have received angelic warnings that allowed them to save the lives of their children. In some cases, people have observed acts of intervention by the angels themselves, and have seen benevolent beings of light performing actual physical rescues of children.

An "Awesome Being"
Saved Her Daughter from a Fiery Death

Reverend L. Larson told of a woman in his congregation, Myrna Martinson, who was awakened from sleep by a beautiful spirit being who told her to pray. She did as she was bade and continued in earnest prayer for an hour or more. At last a feeling of tranquility came over her, and she fell back asleep.

A few hours later, Mrs. Martinson was awakened from her sleep once again— the second time by a startling telephone call that informed her that at the very time she had been praying, her nine-year-old daughter, Tammy, who was away in the city visiting her grandparents, was trapped in their burning home.

The fireman who rescued the girl said that he had found the child's bedroom completely enveloped in flames—except for the corner in which Tammy crouched. Standing protectively over the girl, the fireman swore, was "an awesome being, all white and silvery," who withdrew at his approach and seemed to turn over the rescue of the girl to his professional firefighter's skills.

Later, after she had spent some time breathing from an oxygen mask, Tammy corroborated the fireman's perceptions of the "awesome" silvery and white being.

"He was my guardian angel," she said simply. "And he protected me from the fire until the big fireman came."

An Angel Kept the Lost Boy
Warm at Night in the Woods

In his book *Heaven and the Angels*, H. A. Baker tells of a five-year-old boy of Angelholm, Sweden, who was lost in the woods for six days while four hundred people searched for him.

When he was at last found, the child said, "At night I looked up to the stars and prayed to God to help me get home again. I often got cold, but whenever I did, an angel would come and put his arms around me to keep me warm."

He Watched an Angel Protect
the Chinese Boy from Falling Bombs

Reverend Carl Swanson, a retired missionary who had served in China just prior to World War II, often spoke of the time when he witnessed repeated acts of angelic intervention on behalf of a twelve-year-old member of his congregation.

"The Japanese were attacking the city on that terrible day," he said, "but I was continually inspired and assured of God's grace—for on three occasions I saw an angel move the lad bodily from places where bombs were about to explode! The boy lived to grow up to become a dynamic Christian minister to his people."

A Heavenly Being Tossed
Rattlesnakes from Their Path

Dr. Eugene Martin of El Paso could never forget the manifestation of the angel of deliverance that appeared on a warm spring day in 1923 when he was a boy of seven making the rounds with his doctor father in a depressed rural area of Texas.

"My father had just delivered a baby for a poor family, and he had declined the two dollars that had been offered to him by the father because of the man's obvious poverty," Eugene said.

"We were headed for home on the back of old Sally, our faithful quarter horse. I sat directly behind Dad, my knees pressed against the saddle and my little hands clutching his coat so I wouldn't fall off."

Suddenly, the horse's body began to quiver, and it began to whinny in a strange manner.

"I remember that I was afraid that we would be bucked off her back if Sally got spooked," he said, "but then I heard my father gasp, 'Dear God, Gene, look!'"

Seven-year-old Gene Martin peered around his father's black-coated torso to perceive a wonderfully beautiful being on the road before them.

"It was human in form with golden hair and a youthful face," Eugene said, completely confident in his memory's image of the extraordinary being. "Its garments were a celestial green, and a soft golden aura enveloped the length of its form.

"The angel did not speak," Eugene Martin noted, "but I felt within the very essence of me that the supernatural being had answered a multitude of questions for me in the God-mirrored glories of its eyes."

Sally once again started walking, and the angel kept pace beside them, moving just a bit ahead of them.

"Suddenly the beautiful being knelt before an old fallen tree that spanned the dirt road and scooped its hand along the opposite side of the rotting trunk. Dad and I both gave a small shout of surprise and shock when the angel tossed three huge rattlesnakes into the bushes at the side of the trail."

Both father and son were coldly aware that if the rattlesnakes had struck at Sally's legs or hooves as she stepped over the fallen tree trunk where they had been sunning themselves on that warm spring day, the old girl would likely have reared back in panic and thrown her riders into the jagged rocks that lined the primitive roadway. They could easily have been killed.

Eugene Martin remembered that he began to tremble and hold his father still tighter. He closed his eyes when he heard his father begin to utter a prayer of thanks—and when he opened his eyes, the angel had disappeared.

"How I wish that everyone who has ever doubted the divine could witness the presence of such a beautiful angelic being," Eugene Martin said. "No one could ever again be materialistic and earthly after having such an experience."

Without attempting to express a sentiment that would seem pretentious, Dr. Martin commented that he had always felt that their lives had been spared because of the many acts of kindness that his father regularly performed for the poor families in the area.

"And I am certain," he concluded, "that the appearance of the heavenly being inspired me in later years to seek in my own medical practice to emulate the model of compassion always exhibited by my father."

An Angel Helped Her Drive Through Heavy Traffic
When Grandpa Had a Heart Attack

Linda Harmitz, twenty-eight, who lives in a small town in Nebraska, recalled a frightening experience when as a ten-year-old girl she was forced to take the wheel of the car after her grandfather had suffered a heart attack.

"What had begun as a delightful field trip with Grandpa Clifford could have ended in a real tragedy if it had not been for angelic intervention," Linda said. "We had set out early that August morning for Omaha in Grandpa's old Pontiac. He said that he wanted to buy me some back-to-school clothes in one of the big department stores in the city, and I was very excited at the prospect of a shopping trip with my favorite grandfather."

As was Grandpa Clifford's habit, they had to stop for coffee a couple of times on the way, so it was nearly noon by the time they were approaching downtown Omaha.

"We were stopped at a busy intersection, waiting for the traffic light to change to green, when Grandpa started making this terrible moaning sound," Linda recalled. "The green light flashed on, and Grandpa was driving across the intersection, when he suddenly clutched at his chest and toppled over on his side, almost on top of me!"

Ten-year-old Linda managed to squirm out from under her grandfather's body, and she grabbed for the wheel.

"I had only watched adults drive," she said. "Obviously at age ten, I had never even sat behind the wheel when the motor was running. What was worse, though, was the fact that Grandpa's right foot was wedged up against the accelerator, and we were moving through traffic at a pretty good clip."

Horns blared all around her, and Linda could hear the angry squeal of brakes as other drivers swerved their automobiles to miss Grandpa's wayward Pontiac.

"I tried to get more directly behind the wheel and to move Grandpa's foot away from the accelerator," Linda remembered. "I didn't know what was wrong with Grandpa, but I had overheard Mom worrying about his heart troubles. The only thing I knew for certain was that he was not moving—and I thought we would both soon be killed in traffic."

And then Linda found herself praying at the top of her voice. "Please, God, oh, please, help me get through this traffic and park the car! And if you're too busy just now, *please* send an angel to help me!"

The words were scarcely out of her mouth when the ten-year-old girl felt a touch on her right shoulder and two luminous hands reached over and took hold of the steering wheel.

"I was more than happy to surrender Grandpa's Pontiac to their charge," Linda said. "I remembered a verse from the Bible that I had heard in Sunday school about 'the angels shall have charge concerning thee,' so I just shouted out: 'Thank you, dear angel, *take charge!*'"

And, according to Linda Harmitz and her adult recollections of the remarkable experience, "those skillful hands guided the car safely through the traffic, down a side street, and onto an empty lot next to a service station."

The moment the danger was passed and the Pontiac was out of the heavy traffic flow, the two softly glowing hands disappeared and Linda reached down to turn off the ignition.

"I rolled down the window to scream for help," Linda said, "but an alert attendant had noticed that a very small person had appeared to drive a very large car onto the lot next to their service station, and he was already on the run toward our Pontiac. When he saw Grandpa sprawled on the front seat, he yelled at another man at the station to call an ambulance."

Linda's grandfather had suffered a heart attack, but it was not fatal. "He lived another six years," she said. "Long enough for him to tell everyone he knew the story of how his bold ten-year-old granddaughter had taken over the wheel when he had passed out and how she had managed to drive through heavy traffic to the safety of a vacant lot right next to a service station."

Rejecting any claims of personal glory, Linda insisted on telling her version of the story exactly the way it had happened: The hands of an angel who heard her prayer took over the driving of the car.

"I was frightened out of my mind," Linda admitted. "And the honking car horns, squealing brakes, and motorists' curses only confused me all the more. Those were the capable hands of my guardian angel that took the wheel that day in Omaha—not the trembling little hands of a nearly hysterical ten-year-old girl. I will cherish the memory of this childhood experience until, one day, I join the angels myself."

Big Al, the Guardian Angel with Muscles

On the nights after school when Roy Lee Jefferson and his younger brother, Jackie, used to play basketball in the park of a Detroit suburb, they would pass by a life-size statue of a guardian angel with its hands resting on the shoulder of a young boy.

"Almost every night when we went by the statue," Roy Lee said, "Jackie would smile up at the angel and say, 'Wouldn't it be nice to know that we had a big dude like that watching over us? Wouldn't it be great if angels really did exist?'

"That was back in 1969. I was thirteen at the time, and Jackie was nine," Roy Lee continued.

The park commission had set up a number of individual basketball hoops and four complete courts in the park, and Roy Lee and Jackie played there often. They normally encountered a number of boys and young men playing teams, one-on-one, or just practicing throws.

"There were also some punks that hung around, just trying to look tough," Roy Lee said. "Sometimes they would play a game with some of us, but most of the time it just seemed as though they were waiting for a chance to shake us down and rob us of whatever money we might have on us."

The acknowledged superstar of the hoops at the park was Albert Oakes, a local basketball hero who had been out of high school six or seven years. When he was in school, everyone had expected him to go on to play for a Big Ten college and become a famous professional basketball star. The entire community had felt the effects of the tragedy when Albert and his girlfriend, Opal Hendrickson, were in an automobile accident on the night of their senior prom. Opal was killed, and Albert's hopes for a career as a pro basketball player were ended.

Oakes got a job in a local factory as soon as he recovered from the immediate effects of the accident, since he knew there was no chance of a college scholarship if he would never again be a superstar on the court. He released his stresses, tensions, and sorrows at the park on Mondays, playing basketball with his buddies on his one night off.

"Big Al was heavily muscled, as well as being tall, and all of us kids looked up to him as 'The Man,'" Roy Lee said. "To us, he looked to be about seven feet tall. He was probably around six four or so, but, man, did he look big to us kids, like a giant. We always thought that he was well named, 'Oakes,' because to us he was as big and as tall as an oak tree."

The incident that changed the lives of Roy Lee and Jackie occurred on a cold Thursday evening in late October.

"Jackie insisted that he wanted to go shoot some hoops after supper," Roy Lee said. "I tried to talk him out of it because it was so cold." Roy Lee was also worried about the hoods. Even though there might not be many guys on the courts because of the cold, a chilly night wouldn't do anything to deter the mean-eyed punks from hanging around the park, looking for victims.

But Roy Lee finally gave in to the pleas of his kid brother, and they set out for the park right after supper.

"I remember when we walked past the statue of the guardian angel, I said to myself, 'Hey, angel, I hope you are on duty, watching out for us tonight,'" Roy Lee said.

When they arrived, the two brothers saw that they had the courts to themselves.

Roy Lee tried to persuade Jackie to leave, but the stubborn nine-year-old insisted on practicing his free throws when no one would push him down or jump in front of him. Jackie seemed completely oblivious to the three boys in their midteens who were walking toward them.

Before Roy Lee could grab Jackie by the arm and steer him off the court and out of the park, the three young toughs were on them.

"I just bet these boys got some money on them," said the largest of the trio.

"No money. No nothing," Roy Lee said, shaking his head. "We don't want any trouble."

The big one, the apparent leader of the group, laughed. "I'll just bet you don't want trouble. Well, we don't want trouble either. We just want your money."

"Let us go!" Jackie shouted. "We haven't done anything to bother you. And we don't have money."

The big thug laughed again, this time at Jackie's plea. "Listen to the little mama's boy cry. Hey, little boy, you want your mama to come help you?"

Just then, a tall, bulky figure appeared behind the three punks. "What are you boys doing here? Get out of here and leave these two alone."

"I saw that it was Big Al," Roy Lee said. "But it was a *Thursday night*. Albert had only Monday nights off. I didn't know how he came to be here on a Thursday night, but I was sure glad to see him."

Albert towered over the hoods, well over a head taller than the largest of the three. And he probably weighed more than all of them put together.

"Did you punks hear me?" he roared. "These courts are for athletes, not for bums like you. Get out of here. *Now!*"

The young hoodlums decided that discretion—and a hasty retreat—was the better part of valor against an angry giant, so they left the courts at a run.

Jackie leaned against Roy Lee and let out a sigh of relief. The brothers hugged each other, then turned to thank Big Al.

He was nowhere to be seen.

"It was as if he had vanished," Roy Lee said. "We decided that he must have been walking by, saw that we were in trouble, came to our rescue, and then left again.

"But we couldn't figure out how he could have disappeared so quickly. It seemed impossible that anybody so big could move so fast that he could vanish from sight in a matter of seconds!

"But we decided that we had better not stand around any longer trying to solve the mystery of Big Al's incredible vanishing act. It seemed wisest to leave for home and not take any more chances that night."

The next week on Monday night the weather was milder and the courts in the park were full.

Roy Lee and Jackie walked over to the court where Albert Oakes and his buddies were warming up to play a team from another neighborhood.

When the two brothers thanked Al for saving their skins on Thursday night, he didn't know what they were talking about.

"You guys know that I work every night but Monday." Al frowned down at them from his great height. "It couldn't have been me on Thursday night. I was working in the factory. I wasn't anywhere near here."

"But we saw you here, Big Al," Jackie told him. "You saved our tails from those guys."

"Wasn't me, kid." Al grinned. "Must have been some other guy."

When the brothers persisted, Big Al became impatient with them. "You boys know that Monday night is my *only* night off. That is the way it has been for seven years now—and it isn't likely to change for another seven. Now, excuse me, but I've got a game to win here."

"Jackie and I knew that we had both seen Big Al Oakes at the courts on that Thursday night," Roy Lee said. "And it was for darned sure that the three punks who were about to beat us up saw him.

"On the way home that night, we stopped by the statue of the guardian angel in the park, and we both had the same thought at the same time: Our guardian angel had taken the shape of Albert Oakes to frighten away those punks.

"When we talked about this to Gram Jefferson later, she said that there were no hard and fast rules that said that angels always had to appear with wings and such. She said that an angel could take any form that it needed to in order to perform its mission on Earth.

"Anyway," Roy Lee concluded, "Jackie and I knew that it was our guardian angel who came to our rescue that night in the shape of Big Al Oakes."

Rescued from a Blinding
Mountain Blizzard by an Angel

Although the vast majority of percipients of angelic interaction with children describe the entities as beautiful of countenance, clothed in brilliant white garments, and sheathed in dazzling illumination, many people describe more earthy angels—which any of us might encounter while completely unaware.

DOUGLAS HANKS, THIRTY-FOUR, of Colorado Springs, Colorado, believes that he and twenty others owe their lives to an angel who mysteriously appeared and disappeared when he was a fifteen-year-old guide caught in a sudden Rocky Mountain blizzard.

"My father started taking me along on mountain hikes and climbs when I was barely three years old," Hanks said. "Without wishing to sound egotistical, I was a strong climber and nearly inexhaustible hiker by the time I was thirteen.

"In the summer of 1974, an entrepreneurial friend of Dad's decided that he wanted to create a wilderness camp that would give big-city kids from the concrete canyons the chance to experience some real Rocky Mountain highs. To make it even more appealing for the kids, he wanted to hire a bunch of youthful counselors and guides instead of sending them packing on the trail with grizzled old mountain-man types. True to form, Dad generously volunteered my services for the season to help his friend launch his new enterprise."

Hanks remembered well that he and two other teenage guides had taken a group of eighteen kids—aged nine to twelve, eleven boys and seven girls—on a mountain trail for an afternoon hike.

"We were really very high when we were suddenly caught in a violent blizzard. This would have been frightening enough with experienced hikers, but with eighteen little greenhorns from the city, it was every mountain guide's worst nightmare."

Accepting the grim fact that at the age of fifteen he was the senior guide, Hanks realized that it was really up to him to get everyone safely down the mountain trail to the main camp.

"We really had no choice other than to head back down," he said. "We had no tents, no blankets, no intention of camping out. This was a completely unseasonal storm. It might have been all melted away in two days—but by that time we could all have been dead."

Hanks divided the main body of hikers into three groups of six, each one led by one of the teenage counselors.

"Dean Rafferty was another fairly well-experienced fifteen-year-old," he recalled. "Phil Lobano was seventeen, but he had never spent any time at all in the mountains. He had been chosen as a counselor based on his talents as a folk singer and banjo player."

Hanks arranged it so the best and the strongest of the children were in two groups. He took the six weakest and most inexperienced of the kids with him, four girls and two boys. "Thank God, we had thought ahead to take some rope with us," he said. "And thankfully we had enough so that each of us leaders could tie our kids to us in connecting loops, just like mountain climbers, so that we would be able to keep each group together.

"The snow was coming down in that hard, almost sandlike variety that really tears at the eyes," Hanks recalled. "And the wind was deadly on the breath at that altitude. I knew we had to move out of the blizzard area as fast as we could."

They were not many minutes into their retreat when Hanks began to regret his decision to take the weakest of the party with him. All of the children were crying in fear and confusion. The smallest boy kept stumbling and falling, and instead of helping him to his feet, the other kids had a tendency to keep walking and dragging him along—without notifying Doug that one of their group was down.

As they were working their way around a jutting boulder in a narrow area of the path, two of the kids went toppling over the side.

"Thank heaven I had thought to link us together with the rope," Hanks said. "For without the rope binding us together when they fell, they would have dropped thousands of feet—to their certain death.

"But I began to worry about the next narrow passageway. If three or four of the kids should fall off the path at the same time, I didn't know if I had the weight or the strength to keep the rest of us secure. We might all go plummeting over the edge. The way my group was stumbling and falling every few feet, we just might beat everyone down the mountain—the hard way!"

Douglas Hanks was praying for a nice warm cave or some other miracle, when he heard a voice shout, "Hey, guys. Steady now!"

He was astonished to see very dimly in the whipping snow an anchorman at the other end of the rope—a husky, broad-shouldered kid who was bracing his feet solidly against a jut of rock. The rope grew taut as the stumbling children's weight tugged at it, but the anchorman's added strength helped to hold the group firmly on the narrow ledge. Hanks' own grip grew stronger, and he demanded that the kids stop screaming in panic and watch their step on the treacherous trail.

"In the violently swirling snow there was no way that I could make out the face of the anchorman at the other end of the rope," Hanks said. "My only thought at the time was just getting the kids safely down the mountain. I figured that either Dean or Phil had recognized the foolishness of my bravado in taking all the weaker kids with me and had selected one of the stronger hikers from his group and sent him to add an eighth member to my cluster of stumbling, crying greenhorns. I just didn't recall any of our kids being that big and bulky."

Hanks will not hesitate to proclaim the grim truth that his group of six children would probably never have made it down the mountain trail that night in the terrible storm if it had not been for the unknown anchorman.

"Yes," Hanks emphasized, "I have to say 'unknown,' because by the time we reached a plateau of safety where the adult sponsors of the camp were waiting for us in vans and station wagons, the eighth loop that had been tied around the waist of my mysterious anchorman was dragging empty. That anchor of strength had become a roped ring of nothingness."

Hanks, the other two teen counselors, and the three adult sponsors counted noses. All eighteen greenhorn campers were present and accounted for. There were no extra kids—and thank God, none less!

"Both Phil and Dean and the kids within each of their groups had noticed the eighth member of my team, and they all commented on his surefootedness and his apparent strength and bulk. Since all members of the other two groups were visibly present within their own rope loops, everyone wondered where the 'extra kid' had come from.

"Another strange aspect of our mysterious anchorman was that no one could remember seeing him leave."

For nearly twenty years now, Doug Hanks has expressed his sincere belief that the unknown anchorman who enabled him to get all the kids to safety was an angel.

"Just before the angelic anchorman materialized, I was about to start crying louder than any of the frightened little greenhorns," he admitted. "After all, I was just a fifteen-year-old kid who was doing his best to act bravely and responsibly. I know that that angel with muscles was the answer to my prayers that stormy night on the mountain."

Her Guardian Angel Put a Halt to the Abuse from Her Alcoholic Father

Jenny Radovich, a twenty-one-year-old college student from Wilmington, Delaware, told us that she had endured an abusive childhood that eventually progressed to her father's crude attempts at incest. And then one incredibly wonderful evening, a miracle occurred.

"To say that our home life was imbalanced when I was a child would be putting it mildly," she said. "As early as I can remember, my father drank too much. When we were lucky, he fell asleep in front of the television set. When we were unlucky, he would first beat Mama, then my brother, Billy, then me. It was like a kind of terrible ritual."

When Jenny reached the age of eleven, however, her abusive father began to look at her with a perverse awareness that she might provide him with a more satisfactory outlet for his hostilities than a simple beating.

"One night after he had finished beating Mama and Billy, Pa suddenly grabbed me by the arm and pulled me after him into my bedroom," Jenny said. "I just figured that I was going to get a really terrible beating all alone in my room, but then I saw him fumbling with the fly of his trousers.

"Thank God, Pa was too drunk to finish what he had started that night, but the partially successful act of incest was very ugly and upsetting to me. I got sick to my stomach when I realized that this would probably be a terrible new part of the ritual of abuse."

Although Jenny got pulled into the bedroom by her father on many other occasions, each time her prayers were answered as he either fell asleep or was unable to complete the act due to the effects of the alcohol.

One night, as soon as she had twisted free of her father's drunken hands, Jenny ran from the house and took refuge in the Baptist church two blocks away from their home.

"I sat in the back pew. I was all alone in the church, and I knew that I had to pray and ask God for strength. I wanted to run away from home, but I knew that I was really too young to survive in the streets—and besides, I couldn't leave Mama and Billy to the drunken mercies of Pa."

After a few moments of prayer, Jenny was startled to see an angel standing in the aisle next to her.

"At first I was scared to death of him," she said. "I thought maybe it was the Angel of Death. And then I thought that maybe I was somehow to blame for Pa's wanting to have sex with me."

Jenny was astonished when the angel moved into the pew and sat down beside her. "When he looked at me, all fear just melted away.

"Then he began to talk to me. Not with his mouth, but with his mind. He spoke of many things that I cannot remember, but I just rejoiced in the love that I felt emanating from him. And I clearly remember that he told me to go home and not to be afraid anymore."

Three nights later, Jenny's father was again wholly involved in the ugly process of becoming drunk and increasingly mean. On this night of miracles, however, there were no more beatings.

"Pa started toward Mama, and I remember that I shouted at him to stop,"

Jenny said. "He turned to me with that same awful look that came over him when he pulled me into my bedroom, and he started to stagger toward me.

"That was when this brilliant ball of blinding light came right through the window and hovered over me. Believe me, that light was so bright that none of us could more than glance at it for a few seconds at a time.

"Then we all heard this deep voice speaking from the light: 'Jacob Radovich, change your life tonight. Change your life or lose your soul!'

"Pa fell to the floor in a dead faint. The brilliant light spun around the room three times, then disappeared. When Pa came to, he began to cry like a baby. Mama hugged him, and we all started to cry.

"After a few minutes, Pa got to his feet and poured a six-pack of beer and two bottles of whiskey down the kitchen sink. Mama kissed us kids and said that an angel had just brought back the man that she had married.

"She was right," Jenny said. "To my knowledge, Pa never took another drink, and I know that he never raised a hand to Mama and us kids again. He died in his sleep four years later, and we all felt that he went to heaven with his soul intact."

An Angel's Demand for Another Photo
Saved a Child and Her Family from Certain Death

In the spring of 1951, when Caroline Austman was five years old, she was visiting California's famous Bear Cave with her family. Little Caroline had ventured just a bit apart from her parents and her brother, and was about to rejoin them to go home, when a voice like a "crystal bell" spoke to her: *Tell them to take another picture before they leave.*

"I looked up to see a beautiful figure with long, flowing hair who was dressed in a silvery robe," Caroline recalled. "Although the incident occurred more than forty years ago, I shall never forget the sight of that lovely light being."

As the child stood stunned before the magnificent entity, the angel's compelling eyes and forceful voice reinforced its command:

It is very important that you mind me, Caroline. Tell your mother and father that they must take another picture of Bear Cave before they leave!

In spite of the fact that her family was already in their station wagon, the five-year-old began to insist that one more picture be taken of the cave.

"We've already taken most of a roll of pictures, honey," her mother told her. "Please get in the car now. It's time to go home."

"I don't know why I didn't tell them about the beautiful entity that appeared to me in the cave," Caroline said. "Somehow I felt that the angel's materialization and his firm instructions were supposed to be just my secret. But I continued to obey its orders that we must take another snapshot before we left the park."

Caroline refused to budge from the cave entrance. "Just one more picture, *please?*"

The little girl could plainly see her father's jaws clamping down hard on his pipe stem. She had long ago learned that the tightening of his jaw muscles was a sure indication that she was overstepping boundaries.

"That's enough now, Caroline," he said in the authoritarian voice that she would later hear him use with the men who worked for him in his construction company. "Get into the car right now."

"Not until you take one more picture of us, Daddy," Caroline answered, standing her ground, totally obeying the orders of the heavenly visitor, "*Please, Daddy.*"

"You are such a spoiled brat," Timmy, her nine-year-old brother, accused her. "You can be such a little jerk."

"Timmy, no name-calling," Mother scolded.

But Caroline could see that Mommy was thinking similar thoughts. To this day, Caroline cannot imagine how she managed to escape her rigid display of stubbornness without a few swats on her bottom, but she continued to beg and whine until the family acquiesced to her pleas and climbed out of the station wagon for one more snapshot of Bear Cave.

"The time involved in the taking of this one additional picture had, of course, caused a delay in our leaving the park," Caroline said. "We had not driven very far, when we came upon the scene of a terrible three-car accident.

"Since Mom was a nurse, she got out of the station wagon and asked the highway patrolman if she could be of any assistance. She was told an ambulance was on the way, but it appeared to the officer that most of the seven passengers were already dead.

"I had never seen my mother so pale, and her hands were trembling when she whispered to Daddy that from what the trooper had told her—about the time the accident occurred and all—we would certainly have been involved if we had left the park when they had intended.

"'If we hadn't given in to Caroline's fussing for one more picture,'" I heard Mom tell Dad, "'we could all have been killed in that dreadful accident.'"

Since that time, Caroline added, she has heard the voice of the angelic figure on many occasions.

"Once, unknown to me, my father had been bitten by a poisonous scorpion. The 'crystal voice' told me even before I had heard of the incident that Dad would be all right," she said. "When I look back over things that have happened to me, I must say that I have been guided and comforted by my crystal-voiced angel through the major crises of my life."

Her Angels Promised Always to Be with Her and to Make Her "Indestructible"

Contesa Gypsy Amaya of Santurce, Puerto Rico, said that when she was a little girl traveling with her parents in the circus, she would often communicate with her angels, who appeared to her as "young, lovely ladies." The heavenly beings always smiled at her and promised her that throughout her life they would be near to take care of her.

"Many times my angels came to me," she remembered. "And although I was born nearly blind, they continued to work with me until I could see. The doctors were very puzzled by this, because they had said that I would never be able to see well."

Gypsy's father was a Romany Gypsy from Bessarabia, and her mother was an Egyptian. In spite of two such exotic parents, she was born in Milwaukee, Wisconsin, where her father was appearing as a bandmaster.

She was only thirteen when she began to play the accordion in restaurants and at private parties. As Gypsy Markoff (her maiden name), she appeared in hundreds of USO performances for the GIs in the Second World War.

"One time the angels really helped me when I was an adult and was on the USO tour with the singer Jane Froman in 1943," Contesa Amaya said. "As we were landing in Lisbon, Portugal, our airplane crashed into the Tagus River. I had never learned to swim, but I felt my angels supporting me in the water.

"I had a broken shoulder, a broken collarbone, and I was bleeding very, very badly. I had thoughts that if there were sharks in the water, they would smell the blood and would surely take me. It was very frightening.

"But then I had my vision of the lovely angels telling me that everything would be all right. The beautiful angels stilled my terror.

"Then out of nowhere came a light, and some fishermen found us. Out of the thirty-nine people on board, twenty-four lost their lives."

Contesa Amaya shared yet another story of an angelic rescue, which occurred on Christmas Eve, 1945. The promise that her angels had made to her as a child was still very much in effect. "I was again with a group of USO entertainers in

Kobe, Japan. I had just gone to bed, and I was dozing, when I saw this beautiful lady standing beside my bed.

"She told me to get up, and she held out her hand to pull me out of bed. Her hand was very solid. I started to dress and she handed me my clothes.

"Then I noticed the chandelier begin to swing. The whole building started to shake. I had no sooner gotten out of my room, when the ceiling collapsed. I ran through the streets, following the beautiful lady. All around me buildings were falling down and being demolished.

"Finally we reached a doorway, where she told me to stay. Then she disappeared. I stood there safe, completely clothed against the cold; but I had forgotten to put on my shoes. I developed pneumonia, and I was taken to Tokyo General Hospital.

"General Douglas MacArthur came to see me in the hospital and called me the 'indestructible Gypsy.' But I know that it has been my angels that have made me so indestructible."

C H A P T E R   3

Heavenly Benefactors

Warm Blankets and
Christmas Money from an Angel

ERRIE RIGGS AND JULIE WILKINS believe firmly that the benevolent
stranger who brought them blankets and money when they were
young girls in North Dakota was an angel.

It was in November 1964. They were the Oltersdorf sisters then.
Julie was fourteen and Merrie was ten.

"We were living in an old farmhouse that seemed to have more cracks than
Daddy could patch with tar paper," Julie remembered. "We had lost our farm the
year before, and we lost Mama to typhoid fever that summer.

"There were four of us kids—Steve, twelve, and Karl, eight, besides us two
girls—who had to snuggle next to the old oil burner in the front room and try
to keep warm enough to do our homework at night."

It was just after Thanksgiving when Merrie came down with a terrible fever.
The kids had but one blanket apiece, but they all piled the covers on Merrie
when they were doing their chores or their homework. Normally, they walked
around the old farmhouse with blankets wrapped around them to ward off the
cold, but they wanted Merrie to get warm enough to break her fever.

Since late October, their father, Gus, had been working at the grain elevator in town. During planting and harvest, he had been a hired man for Miles Hanson, but the elderly farmer had no need for help during the winter months. The Oltersdorf family, however, still had need for food, regardless of the season, so Gus worked at the elevator.

Julie remembered that their father was really depressed. It would be their second Christmas without the farm—and their first Christmas without Mama.

"We used to have really nice Christmases," she said. "We were never rich, but we were well enough off until Daddy had that run of bad luck. But, of course, more than our nice home and the presents, we would miss Mama terribly."

All the children noticed the deep melancholy that had possessed their father, so Merrie had not wanted to concern him with her illness. She knew that he had enough on his mind with the bills and all.

"I lay and prayed for one solid day while the other kids were at school," Merrie said. "I prayed that we could have some more blankets and just a little extra money so that we could have a nicer Christmas and so Daddy would not have to work so hard."

MERRIE WAS LYING next to the oil burner that afternoon when she saw her angel. She knew that her fever was getting higher, and she so wanted Julie near her. Julie was the oldest and, just like Mama, always seemed to know what to do.

Merrie was startled to hear the door open, for she knew that Julie had locked it when she and the boys left for school that morning. Merrie was even more surprised when she turned to see a "beautiful man" walk into the house.

"He was fairly tall, well built, and I will always remember his long blond hair and his bright blue eyes," Merrie said. "I started to say something about trespassing, but he smiled and lifted a hand in a friendly way that seemed to say 'I won't hurt you.'

"He had four thick blankets under his arm, and he set them down on the kitchen table. For the first time I noticed that he wore hardly anything at all against the terrible November cold. He wore no coat, just a thin white shirt and blue jeans. I knew that he meant to give us those blankets, so I spoke up and said: 'You had better keep those for yourself, mister. You'll freeze to death in this cold climate.'

"I've always thought it interesting," Merrie said, "that young as I was—just ten going on eleven—I somehow felt that he had come from some warmer place. That was why I said 'climate.'"

The stranger smiled again and spoke for the first time—in a voice that sounded as if he were singing and talking at the same time. "I won't need the blankets. They are for you."

Just before the blond stranger left, he took five twenty-dollar bills from inside his shirt and set them on top of the blankets. "You'll be better soon, Merrie," he said as he walked out the front door.

After he had gone, Merrie was convinced that she had seen an angel. "I just knew that the stranger was the angel that I had prayed for to come and help us," she said. "And I will believe that until the day I die. And then I know that I will see him again."

Julie resumed her account of the incident:

"When we got home from school, we found the front door locked just as we had left it, so we were really surprised when Merrie told us that someone had walked in on her that afternoon. And when she said that an *angel* had brought us kids each a new blanket and some money for Daddy, I felt her brow and got really scared. Her fever felt so hot. We covered her with those new blankets—

wherever they had come from—and poured steaming hot tea down her throat until the fever broke.

"Daddy always felt that some nice young man in town or on one of the neighboring farms had learned of our plight and had given us the blankets and the money," Julie said. "One hundred dollars might not seem like much today, but in 1964 it was just enough to give Daddy the buffer he needed to get caught up with some bills, and he was even able to afford some Christmas presents for us.

"We kids always believed Merrie," Julie stated. "Even then she was a good artist, and she was able to draw a really good picture of the benevolent stranger. We had lived in that community all of our lives, and we lived there another eight years—and none of us ever saw anyone who looked the way he did.

"I agree with my sister that an angel helped us survive that terrible winter of sixty-four."

An Angel Protected
Her Tuition Money for Music Camp

For many years, Sharon Olson has been a highly respected Midwestern musician who emphasizes inspirational and religious music in both her professional expression as a performer and in her classes as a teacher at a denominational college. She has directed both vocal and instrumental groups, and she herself has been a featured vocalist in such choral presentations as Handel's *Messiah* and has performed as a solo flutist with symphony orchestras.

"Even as a child I knew that I must express my love of God through music," Sharon said. "I felt that the Holy Spirit had touched me in this way and had given me a special gift that I must realize to its fullest expression in musical service to God's glory."

As she evaluates the development of her artistic career, Sharon can easily isolate one event as pivotal in her evolution as a musician. "When I was fourteen years old, I was chosen to study at a summer music camp sponsored by our church. It was here that I first met some of the great teachers who provided me with the inspiration I needed in order to see beyond the shuttered restrictions and walled-in boundaries of my doubts, fears, and insecurities, and to perceive that music has the power to liberate the spirit and allow it to encompass the universe."

Sharon is quick to add that she might never have been able to undergo that crucial church music camp experience if it had not been for the ministrations of an angel.

"In order to be able to attend the camp, I had to have a certain amount of tuition money to match the stipend provided by our local church," Sharon said. "Although the sum was not a large one, in that summer of 1973 almost any amount would have been too much for Dad and me to raise.

"And when we did at last manage to come up with it, we might have lost it all if it had not been for the angel that appeared to me the night before I left for camp."

SHARON REMEMBERS THAT it was an extremely hot July evening with exceedingly high humidity.

"Dad had opened all the doors and windows, and he sat before the kitchen table, perspiration dripping off his forehead as he counted the money for my tuition one more time, 'just to make sure.'"

In order to acquire the extra money that was required to meet their half of the tuition, Dennis Olson had worked as much overtime as his manager at the supermarket in Milwaukee would allow, and now he slumped before the kitchen table in a state of near-total exhaustion.

Life had not been easy for the Olsons for the past four years. In 1969, when Sharon was ten, her mother was terribly injured in an automobile accident, which, to add to the tragedy, was Mrs. Olson's fault.

Janet Olson, strong, athletic, always a fighter, lingered in a painful dimension between partial consciousness and complete coma for more than two years before she succumbed and surrendered to death. By that time all of the insurance policies and all of the Olsons' savings had long been devoured by the insatiable hunger of the medical system.

The Olsons lost the suit brought against them by the other driver in the accident that cost Janet Olson her life, and their nice home had to be sold to meet court costs. Sharon and her father had been forced to rent a small home in what would charitably be described as a "less exclusive" neighborhood.

Even then their bad luck was not over. Dennis Olson was fired from his executive position because of the number of days absent from the workplace due to his wife's accident and the subsequent court case, and he had to scramble to get a job as assistant produce manager at a supermarket.

"Dad had counted out the money that we needed for my tuition in neat piles on the kitchen table," Sharon recalled. "I was really nervous, because there had been a lot of break-ins and burglaries in the neighborhood that summer, and I thought it might be really tempting to some 'weaker brethren' who might just happen to glance in our open windows and see all that money lying there for the taking."

Dennis Olson had poured himself a stiff shot of bourbon, for "medicinal purposes" and "to ward off the heat." He seldom drank, even socially, until after his wife's death.

Sharon did not judge him, but she hoped that he would not fall asleep at the kitchen table, then stumble into bed without locking the doors and windows.

"Dad," she said after she had kissed his forehead, "I've got to be going to bed.

I have to be up early to go to church with the tuition money."

Her father smiled, waved an expansive hand over the piles of bills, carefully sorted according to denominations. "Well, sweetie, it is all here. We did it. You with your babysitting money, and me with my overtime at the supermarket. What a team, eh?"

"The greatest, Dad," she said, hugging him warmly across his shoulders as she stood behind his seated figure. "Thanks, Dad. Thank you so much."

She hated to sound as if she were admonishing him, but she felt that she had to take the chance of offending him in order to protect their hard-earned money.

"Please remember to close and lock all the doors and windows before you come to bed, Dad. We don't want to tempt folks with all that money on the table."

He winked, and made an okay sign with his thumb and forefinger. "Consider it done, my dear. Now run off to bed. I'm going to sit up awhile. Maybe do some thinking. Maybe watch a little news on television."

Sharon lay down on her bed, feeling the warm summer breeze waft over her. Before she drifted off to sleep, she prayed that God would protect her father and herself.

SOMETIME DURING THE NIGHT she was awakened by the touch of a hand on her shoulder shaking her lightly. She opened her eyes. By the light of the moon shining in through the window, she could see that she was alone in her room.

Curious as to what could have awakened her, she got out of bed and peeked into her father's room. He seemed to be sleeping peacefully.

Sharon was puzzled, but also very sleepy. She crawled back into bed, and soon her eyes had closed again and she was once more fast asleep.

Sometime later she was awakened a second time. She was certain that she had felt someone's hand resting lightly on her shoulder. She glanced quickly around her room, once again perceiving that she was completely alone.

"I got to my feet and wearily checked my father's room once more," Sharon said. "It was easy to see that he had not stirred. Then I saw that the hallway was filled with a strange, glowing light. When I turned, I let out a gasp of astonishment—for in the midst of the glowing light stood a beautiful angel!"

Her angel "appeared to be draped in a bright white cloth. His silky white feathery wings were lovely to behold."

The angel's wings, according to Sharon's recollection, were pulled into his side and extended six inches above his shoulder to almost ten inches below his hip. The being's left arm was at his side, but the right one was raised toward her, beckoning her to follow.

"I was so startled at the sight of this beautiful being that I could not move," she said. "But as I stared in wonder at the angel standing in the hallway, he beckoned once more to me."

Uncertain of what was to come, Sharon slowly began to move down the hallway and drew closer to the angelic visitor. Finally, she, too, stood enclosed in the orb of brilliant light that surrounded the angel.

The shield of light followed the two of them, illuminating various rooms in the house as they passed through them. They went into the kitchen, through the dining room, then up to the front door—where the angel suddenly vanished.

The teenager was as startled at being left by the angel as she had been by his sudden appearance. Instinctively she felt for the light switch and turned it on.

"As the quite ordinary electrical light flooded the front room of our house, I could see instantly why the angel had awakened me," Sharon said. "I had prayed to God for protection that night, and now I saw that Dad had forgotten to close and lock the front door. It stood wide open before me. The screen door was unhooked as well."

Sharon whispered a prayer of thanks as she closed and bolted the door. Then she made her way to the rear of the house to check on the back door. She was startled to see that this door was also wide open.

"The pale moonlight clearly illuminated the neat stacks of bills lying on the kitchen table," she recalled. "I closed and locked the back door, and then, summoning all my courage—but secretly feeling that the angel was still somehow rather near—I turned on the lights in the entire house and checked each room to be certain that no one had entered while we slept.

"Once I was completely satisfied that no one lurked in the shadows and that the angel had alerted me to the dreadful situation in time, I scooped all the money in a paper sack and took it with me to bed."

Sharon was convinced that God had answered her prayer to protect her father and herself and that He had sent an angel to alert her to the potential dangers of the night. After composing a heartfelt prayer of thanks, she finally fell into an undisturbed slumber.

"The next morning I was at the church early with my tuition money," Sharon Olson said. "Even at that young age I interpreted the fact that the angel manifested to protect the money as a sign that I would find my destiny and realize my true mission on Earth at the music camp. I have felt protected by our unseen guardians ever since the remarkable experience of that night, and I know that I was led to discover true fulfillment in the inspiration of my ministry of music."

From Childhood to Adulthood, His Angel Was Ever-Present

Leandro Gonzales, who is now sixty-six years old, has stated that he has been conscious of an angelic presence guiding his life path since 1932, when he was a five-year-old boy in Nogales, Mexico.

"I was a very pious child," he said. "One evening after our prayers, I told Mama that I would be a priest.

"As I lay in bed that night, a beautiful angel clothed in a pure white robe appeared to me and said that although I would not be a priest, I would always serve God. The angel also told me that I would always be protected and that I should never worry about things, no matter how awful they might seem."

In 1941, when Leandro was thirteen, the family immigrated to Phoenix, Arizona, where his mother had two sisters. At first it seemed as though life would be much better for them in the United States, but they had lived there only four months when his father was stabbed to death in a dispute with two soldiers outside a bar.

"I had just turned fourteen, but I knew that I was now the man of the family," Leandro said. "I had to take care of my mother and sister. I knew that it was up to me because my aunts' families were very poor and had nothing to spare, and I knew that my mother could not work because of her crippled leg.

"Somehow, even though I was not at all big for my age, I was able to get a job boxing produce for a truck farmer outside the city. Those were the days of manpower shortages during World War Two, and I guess even a scrawny kid like me looked good to a farmer who had to move his product before it spoiled. The trouble was, I had to walk over six miles back and forth to work each day, and I decided to quit going to school."

Gonzales' guardian angel appeared to him and praised him for having gone right out and obtained a job to support his family. But the angel admonished him for having thoughts about quitting school.

"I complained that I was too tired now and that the only way I could continue school was to begin work at four in the morning and, after classes, return to work until eight at night. The angel told me that he would give me all the energy I needed to maintain such a routine," Leandro Gonzales said. "And it was truly amazing how my meager breakfast of a few beans rolled in a tortilla could give me such power. I had begun to believe that my angel was sprinkling it with special food, like the manna from heaven that God gave Moses and the children of Israel in the desert."

By the time Leandro was sixteen, the truck farmer had promoted him to foreman. As soon as he could get a license to drive a truck, he was making deliveries. When Leandro was barely nineteen, the farmer made him a partner in a produce store that he had opened in the city.

"It was also at that time that my angel appeared and told me I should soon think of taking a wife," Gonzales revealed. "That night I had a dream of a beautiful girl with long, dark hair and big, beautiful brown eyes; and when I awakened the next morning, I heard a voice say, 'Her name is Maricela.'"

To his astonishment and total delight, among his first customers that Saturday morning was the Nazarro family, whose members included a beautiful seventeen-year-old daughter named Maricela, who had long, dark hair and very large brown eyes.

"I wanted to tell her as soon as we met that she would be my wife," Gonzales said, "but I waited until our third date. Maricela pleased me so by saying that she had known that I would be her husband the first day we met in the produce store."

Leandro and Maricela married in October 1948, when he was twenty-one and she was nineteen. Their angelically arranged union brought three souls into earthly flesh forms, each one named prior to birth by Leandro's guardian angel.

Under the direction of his angel, Gonzales expanded his enterprise to include a Mexican restaurant, which featured Maricela's authentic family recipes. The unpretentious eating place became so popular among both the Anglo and Latino citizens of Phoenix that Leandro and Maricela were soon able to open two other dining establishments.

"Always my angel has directed me away from dangerous or unsound business decisions," Gonzales testified. "Each morning he comes to me at three o'clock and awakens me to pray."

Gonzales said that his angel often prompts him to give generous sums of money to specific charities.

"Maricela and I have never suffered on account of our gifts," he stated. "Rather, we have become more prosperous. We began tithing ten percent to our church, but now we give twenty percent of our earnings to the Lord's house—and we receive increased abundance from the angels."

In 1970 Gonzales was informed by his angel that his son Lorenzo, who was in the armed services in Vietnam, was in great peril. He was instructed that he must pray all night.

Before dawn he saw his angel clad in white with a countenance "admirable and lovely to behold." When the angel told him the danger to Lorenzo had passed, Gonzales and Maricela went to the church to light candles and to offer prayers of thanks.

Three weeks later Gonzales received a letter from his son telling him of the close call that he had experienced while on patrol in the jungle near their base in Vietnam. "I know that I felt the presence of your angel near me, Dad," Lorenzo wrote. "I pray that he will guide and protect me as he has done for you throughout your entire life."

After he had finished reading his son's letter, Gonzales fell to his knees to offer renewed prayers of thanksgiving, and as he did so, he said that he heard a voice saying, "He that sitteth in the tabernacle of the Most High need never be afraid."

Angelic Visitations Bestow
Gifts of the Spirit on Some Children

Our questionnaire on paranormal and mystical experiences indicates that astonishing numbers of our correspondents received "gifts of the spirit" after their childhood encounters with angels.

Jerry H. of Idaho Falls, Idaho, was left with the gift of precognition after a visitation from a "silvery, silver-haired" angel when he was a boy of eight.

"I can remember so clearly how the angel would appear to me in dreams and tell me things that were about to happen to me or to members of my family," Jerry told us. "Usually these were warnings, things to try to avoid. Sometimes I heard his voice shout warnings to me. I was always glad that I listened to him.

"I still hear him from time to time—especially if there seems to be something really bad lurking ahead in my future."

MAURICE BANKS, A SOCIAL WORKER from Topeka, Kansas, said that after his interaction with a Light Being when he was five or six he was able to hear a warning voice that saved him from danger on several occasions.

"Once it told me to step back just as a heavy piece of glass fell from a high ceiling. It smashed right at my feet," Maurice said. "Twice it saved my life in Korea, when I was in the army.

"Throughout my life the voice has saved me from unpleasant or harmful experiences and guided me to what I later learned were the wisest courses of action."

AS WE STATED EARLIER, ninety percent of the twenty thousand men and women who have responded to our questionnaire have testified that they can clearly recall a visitation from an angelic-type being around the age of five. Subsequent manifestations of gifts of the spirit were evidenced by nearly all our respondents, and we have broken the angelic blessings down in the following manner:

- Thirty-five percent feel that the angel blessed them by healing an aspect of their physical being
- Fifty percent remain convinced that the same angel "watches over them" as a guide or guardian in their adult life
- Ninety percent recall having experienced a sense of oneness with the angel and the universe
- Fifty-five percent report having had a number of intense religious experiences since the initial manifestation of the angel
- Seventy-two percent claim an illumination experience associated with their childhood angelic encounter
- Fifty percent have accomplished dramatic hearings of themselves or others
- Fifty-seven percent have made prophetic statements or experienced prophetic dreams or visions that have come to pass

NEARLY ALL OUR RESPONDENTS who experienced an angelic encounter as a child stated that they were left with a sense of mission. Here is a typical response to our questionnaire:

"It was as if the appearance of the angel somehow served to trigger within me the awareness that I had a mission to perform here on Earth. Even as a small child I'd find myself conforming to this 'programming.' I've always known that there were things that were prohibited for me. I have been programmed to keep my priorities straight. Somehow I am to help the world and other people."

An Angel Visits Summer Camp

It was at summer camp in upper Michigan when she was eight years old that Sherry Steiger underwent such a dramatic physical encounter with an angel that even girls and counselors from neighboring cabins rushed to her bunk to see what had happened.

Sherry Johnson, as she was called then, had been extremely fortunate to have recovered from a life-threatening bout with rheumatic fever. At one point she was not expected to live, but the miracle of many prayers and much penicillin kept her alive.

Sherry had been completely bedridden for nearly a year when the doctor finally pronounced her well enough to get out of bed—until he noticed her bad case of chicken pox, which kept her in bed for several more grueling weeks.

So it was with great glee when Sherry at last was able to go to summer camp. She was still not allowed to swing, slide, or play with the other children, for her heart had been left with a murmur that would have to be carefully monitored.

The night the angel appeared was humid, hot, and still. Everyone was bedded down in their bunks, and the lights were out. Amid the chirp of crickets, an occasional whisper and giggle floated on the gently blowing breeze.

Sherry had just finished her bedtime prayer when she thought someone had turned on the brightest light she had ever seen.

In the corner of the room, at ceiling level, Sherry saw a stream of bluish-white light take on the shape of the most beautiful, gentle, and loving woman imaginable. The "lady" seemed to come through the ceiling, and the brilliant illumination still surrounded her as she hovered with outstretched arms and spoke to Sherry.

The angel delivered a clear message for Sherry and for all the girls present. The beautiful being told them just how very special they each were and how very much God loved them.

The angelic presence was so emphatic in her message that moments later, when Sherry regained a sense of "reality" as to what was going on in the cabin, she looked out from her bunk to see all the girls from her cabin—and from many others—on their knees in a prayerlike position. They all had their eyes affixed to Sherry as if they were somehow expecting the little eight-year-old girl to prompt a longer sermon from the angelic being.

Later, after the angel had disappeared and when Sherry tried to describe all that she had seen and heard to appease the inquisition of the camp counselors, she had tears streaming from her eyes. Looking around, she noticed that many of the other girls were weeping as well.

Some of the girls said that they, too, had seen the angel and saw it speaking to Sherry. Others said that the heavenly light had awakened them—and then they heard Sherry talking and responding to the light being.

From that day forward it seemed as if a plan had been given to Sherry for life. Some sort of an understanding of the sacredness and connectedness of all of God's creatures—a pattern of life that would guide and direct her the rest of her days in ways that she would gradually piece together.

Perhaps some would say that there is little wonder that Sherry had an angel visitation. After all, she was finally freed from a darkened sickroom, and considering the severity of the illnesses and trauma that the little girl had recently undergone, she would most likely be susceptible to such "visions." But no one will ever convince Sherry that the angel she saw was not as real as anyone she has ever seen.

In Answer to His Prayers, an Angel
Found Work for His Unemployed Father

Just as no one can ever convince Mike Shapiro that it was not his prayers as a loving son that summoned the angel who found work for his unemployed artist father.

In 1972, when Mike was eight, his father, Benjamin, a talented artist-cartoonist, suddenly found himself out of a job. "Dad had drawn, inked, and lettered for some of the top names in the syndicated comics," Shapiro said. "Although he had been a successful freelancer for many years, he had decided to take a regular job as a staff artist with a leading national publication when he found out that my sister, Joyce, was on the way. And now, just when he had placed all his financial eggs in one basket, he was summarily fired."

Little Mike's hero was his father. The walls of his room in their Bronx apartment were papered with drawings, sketches, and paintings that his dad had done for some of the biggest titles in the comics business.

"I wanted to be a cartoonist just like Dad," Mike said. "I would sit at my little desk and practice drawing in his style."

It was while he was at his artwork late one Friday afternoon that Mike heard his father delivering the bad news to his mother.

"I can't believe it, Elaine," Dad said. "Just when we were getting used to receiving a weekly paycheck, kaboom! Why did this have to happen now, with the baby on the way?"

His mom tried to console his dad with some words about their savings and the money that she got from her part-time job, but he wasn't accepting any comfort right then.

"You're not going to be able to work that much longer before the baby comes, honey," Dad said. "And our meager savings won't hold out very long either. Let's just hope our money lasts long enough for me to reestablish my connections and start getting freelance work again. Otherwise, I just don't know what we're going to do."

The sound of fear and dismay in his father's voice greatly upset the eavesdropping eight-year-old. "Dad was always so upbeat and so positive. It just broke my heart to hear him feeling so down and so helpless."

Then Mike remembered how he had found himself recently drawing lots of pictures of angels. "I had really been getting into angels. There weren't a whole lot of books on angels back then, so I had asked our rabbi about the heavenly beings. He told me about the angels that appeared to Abraham, the angels that saved Daniel and his friends from the fiery furnace, the angel who wrestled with Jacob, and so on. My brain was bubbling with all of these magnificent stories of angels and their obvious concern with us human beings.

"That's when I decided that I would ask an angel to help find Dad a new job. I remember that I must have prayed all night long."

IT SEEMED STRANGE to find Dad at home after school on Monday. Mom was still at work, so Dad suggested that he and Mike go for a walk.

Even to his youthful sense of direction and order, it seemed to Mike that his father was taking them on a rather erratic route. And when he spoke, his bits of conversation didn't make a whole lot of sense. Mike understood that his father was really troubled about being out of a job.

"We were in a neighborhood that was foreign to us," Mike recalled. "I knew that I had never been there before. But suddenly we were standing in front of this neat little restaurant, and Dad suggested that we go inside and order a sandwich and a soda."

Father and son had just received their sandwiches and sodas from a waitress, when a pleasantly smiling stranger, his hand already resting on the back of Mike's chair, asked if he might join them.

"I knew right away that he was my angel," Shapiro said. "He was well dressed in a blue suit, and he had light blond hair and bright blue eyes. He was a very attractive man with a pleasant, easygoing manner that made you feel good. And Dad, who was normally very reserved and aloof around strangers, just shrugged and said, 'Why not?'"

The man studied father and son for just a few moments, and then said, "I'm sorry to learn about your being fired from your job, Benjamin. It is very difficult when such things occur in life, but you must not be discouraged."

"That cinched it for me," Mike, said. "He had to be my angel. How could a total stranger in a strange neighborhood call Dad by name and know about his losing his job?"

Benjamin squinted at the man over the edge of his glass. "How do you know my name?" he wanted to know. "And how is it you know about my being fired?"

"Oh, I know a lot about you, Benjamin," the man said, giving Mike a knowing wink. "A great deal about you...and your family."

"You must work on the magazine," Benjamin said, believing that he had solved the mystery. After all, he had barely been employed there long enough to become adjusted to the working hours, to say nothing of meeting all the staff members.

The stranger smiled and denied working on the magazine from which Benjamin had just been fired. And then he proceeded to reveal just how much he really did know about the most intimate details of the life of Benjamin Shapiro. After a few minutes, Mike and his father sat mesmerized, their mouths hanging open.

"Then the most amazing thing of all happened," Mike said. "The angel told

Dad where to go for a job. He gave him the address and told him whom to see.

"Next, he gave us both a little inspirational talk about always keeping our chins up and never becoming discouraged. About how we never really walk alone in life. That there's always someone to reach out a helping hand."

Both Mike and his father were so heartened by the man's message and the information about the new job that it took them a moment to realize that the stranger was no longer speaking to them. They looked over their shoulders to see that he was walking out the door.

"I've got to thank him!" Benjamin said, getting to his feet and tossing down some money for the sandwiches and sodas. "I've got to thank him for the tip about the job."

Mike remembered how the two of them ran after the stranger—but when they opened the restaurant door, he was nowhere in sight.

"We had been right behind him," Shapiro said. "We opened the door only seconds after he did—but the stranger had vanished. Dad shook his head and speculated that the guy just blended right in with the people on the street."

Excited by the angel's appearance and disappearance and elated that his prayers had been answered, Mike told his father that the stranger was an angel. "I asked God to send us an angel—and he did!" he exclaimed. "I asked for an angel to help you find a new job—and he came!"

Benjamin laughed at his son's pronouncement. "He was one terrific guy, son, but he was no angel. You didn't see any wings or a halo, did you? He was what you call a mind reader. But, man, he was stupendous, I'll give him that."

That night at dinner, Benjamin told his wife about the incredible psychic that he and Mike had met on their walk. "This guy picked up on everything," he said. "He knew all of our birth dates, where we got married, our anniversary—everything. The guy was fantastic. He could be on the stage, you know, like Dunninger or Kreskin or someone like that."

The next day, Benjamin followed through on the stranger's advice about the job opening. He went directly to the publication the man had recommended. He asked for the specific editor the stranger had suggested, and within the hour he was hired to begin illustrating the issue currently in production.

"Dad often remarked over the next three or four years how he would like to find 'that mind reader' so he could thank him properly," Mike said. "I know that Dad went back to that little restaurant many times, thinking that the man might frequent the place. He described him to the manager, the waiters and waitresses, the cooks, the patrons of the restaurant, but no one claimed to recognize him at all.

"I know that the stranger was my angel, sent to us in answer to my prayers," Shapiro said, concluding his account. "No stranger, no matter how psychically gifted he might be, could have known so much about other human beings and have just the right job advice for my father. No, I know with all my heart and soul that the stranger was the angel that God sent to help Dad find work. And what is more, he winked at me."

Angelic Guides on Near-Death Journeys to Paradise

N 1992, DR. MELVIN MORSE, clinical associate professor of pediatrics at the University of Washington, conducted a study of four hundred people who had survived near-death experiences and concluded that their testimonials constituted proof of life after death.

In his book *Transformed by the Light*, Dr. Morse told the story of Olaf Sunden, who, when he nearly died under surgery at the age of fourteen, returned to life a great deal more intelligent than he was before the near-death experience (NDE). He was immediately transformed from a poor student to one who progressed from the high school honors program to go on to create chemical wonders that ended up making him a multimillionaire.

Dr. Morse also presents the story of a woman who temporarily passed through death's door to meet the child that she had lost at birth years before. During her NDE, an angel informed her that the girl on a nearby swing was the child she had lost.

The woman was hesitant to accept such a revelation because the nurses had taken the stillborn infant away before she had been able to see its sex, so the heavenly being made a point of showing the woman a commalike birthmark on the girl's neck.

When the woman recovered from the injuries she had sustained in an automobile accident, she acquired the autopsy records of her long-deceased child. To her astonishment, she learned that the infant had most certainly been a girl and had the exact same birthmark as the one revealed to her by the angel on the Other Side.

A Message from Alice in the Heavenly Garden

Registered nurse Helen C. was assisting a doctor in the pediatrics section of a county hospital in Tennessee about 1953, when a seven-year-old girl developed serious complications after a relatively minor operation.

The girl lapsed into a comatose state and failed to respond to stimulants. The doctor shook his head sadly, knowing that the child would soon die.

Just as a new day was dawning, however, the girl's eyes flickered open and she called feebly for water.

As a relieved nurse and a joyful mother rushed to the child's bedside, the girl told them of having been in a lovely garden filled with boys and girls.

"It was nice and sunny," the girl informed them, "and all the flowers and bushes were so pretty. The other girls and boys said that they stayed there all the time, but a girl named Alice said that I would have to go back."

As the child chattered on, Nurse Helen C. was suddenly struck by certain words and phrases and wanted to hear more about the girl called Alice.

"Alice wore pigtails with yellow ribbons and her hair was black," the girl told her, pleased to talk more about her experiences in the beautiful garden. "And she said to tell you to give your mother a kiss from her and to let you know that your daddy was all right."

Nurse C. was stunned. She had had a sister named Alice who had died of influenza many years before, when she was seven. Alice had often tied her black pigtails with yellow ribbons. Nurse C.'s father had passed away just three months before this incident.

As soon as she returned home that evening, Nurse C. called her mother and told her that she had received a most wonderful message from Alice in heaven that both she and Daddy were all right. "When Mom asked how I could know such a thing, I told her about the little girl's remarkable journey to a heavenly place. Mom began to cry and said that we had all been blessed."

An Angel Takes a Dying Boy
Beyond the Barriers of Time and Space

Even as a small boy, Brad Steiger accepted the survival of the human spirit as a matter of his faith. But at the age of eleven—after his own near-death experience—he no longer had to be satisfied with a mere "belief" in life after death. From that time forth, he was blessed to "know" that the soul transcends the physical transition of death and that there are benevolent beings who exist to guide us when we are ready to make the adjustment to another plane of existence.

Brad has a fleeting memory of losing his balance, falling off a tractor, and sprawling into the path of the fertilizer spreader's whirling blades.

He remembers pain as the machine's left tire mashed his upper body, and shock as the blades clutched at his head and cut deeply into his flesh and skull.

His world became the color of blood.

Then he was floating about forty feet off the ground, looking down on a tractor and fertilizer spreader somehow brought under control by his seven-year-old sister, June.

Brad was concerned about the mangled farm boy that he saw lying on the hay stubble, yet he was becoming more detached about such matters by the moment.

He seemed strangely unmoved by the scene beneath him. It seemed of only mild importance to him that an eleven-year-old boy was dying in an Iowa pasture.

His real self now seemed to be an orange-colored ball intent on soaring toward a brilliant light.

Strangely, though, his attention seemed to be divided between that wondrous light and an awareness of his father, shocked and in tears, carrying his crumpled body away from the pasture. It seemed as though Brad were physically in his father's arms, bleeding, mangled, dying, and at the same time he was above them, watching the scene as a detached observer.

Then Brad discovered that his Essential Self was free of what he had considered to be the standard confines of Time and Space.

Brad thought of his mother—and instantly he was beside her in the kitchen as she labored over lunch, as yet unaware of his accident.

He thought of his friends with whom he had planned to see the Roy Rogers double feature that night—and immediately he was watching them as they worked with their fathers on their own farms.

That was when it occurred to him that he was dying, and Brad experienced a moment of panic. He did not want to die.

He could not die! He was much too young and had far too many things he wished to accomplish.

It was at that desperately anxious moment that Brad was aware of another presence, a calm, reassuring energy, a being that seemed somehow to be composed of pure light. This energy soothed him and focused his attention on a remarkably beautiful geometric design that somehow instantly conveyed to him that everything was all right.

To behold this fascinatingly intricate, multicolored design was to understand that there was a pattern to the universe.

To perceive its richness and depth was to know that there was meaning to life.

And if it should be his destiny to die at that very moment, Brad's death was also all right and a part of this larger pattern.

Brad's perception of that ineffable design suffused him with a blissful euphoria.

Brad no longer wished to return to that battered and bloody body. He wanted to become one with the beautiful light that shone so brilliantly before him.

But then Brad received a "knowing" that his Earthwalk was not yet completed. There were things to do that lay ahead of him that were far more important than attending cowboy movies.

From a place far away, Brad could hear his father, his uncle, and their family doctor deciding to make a desperate run for a hospital in Des Moines, about 140 miles away, where there was a specialist who might save him—if Brad didn't first bleed to death.

Brad was in and out of the body during those 140 miles, and he did not really come back with any serious intention of remaining in his mangled physical self until the surgery was about to begin.

From his vantage point above the doctors and nurses preparing to operate, it seemed as though that same energy, that same angel, was insisting that he return to his physical body to cooperate in the medical procedure that was about to get under way.

Brad came back with such force that he sat up, shouted, and knocked an intern off balance.

The husky eleven-year-old farm boy began to struggle against the restraining hands of the doctors and nurses, and it took the calming words of a gentle Roman Catholic sister to pacify him until the anesthesia could take effect. Brad had been baptized into the Evangelical Lutheran Church, and nuns had always seemed kind of eerie, mysterious alien figures in their black and white "penguin" outfits, but he clung to the nun's hand and squeezed all the love out of it until he was once again up in a corner of the room.

"I don't want to watch this." Brad remembers pleading with the angel. He was always a bit on the squeamish side when it came to things like blood and doctors' offices. "Please don't make me watch what they are going to do to me."

The angel indicated that it was no longer necessary for Brad's Essential Self to be in the physical body or to look over the surgeons' shoulders during the operation. Brad recalls spending what seemed like a very pleasant day or two in a beautiful park surrounded by happy, friendly, solicitous people of all ages.

When he at last regained consciousness, he looked into the loving eyes of his mother, who hovered nervously at his bedside and clasped one of his hands in her own. His rugged father stood at the foot of the bed, smiling his brave concern.

"I think I was in heaven," Brad whispered in a weak voice. "I think I died and went to heaven. It's a beautiful place, like a big park, with lots of nice people and friendly animals. I think it was an angel who took me there. It was someone bright and shiny, anyway."

At that stage of his creative development, Brad's passion was for sketching. In a few days, after his mother had brought him a set of colored pencils and a drawing pad, he drew a lovely valley surrounded by majestic mountains, alive with animals, with a small village in it, all under the vigilant eye of a watchful guardian astride a great white horse.

"That's kind of what it looked like," Brad told his mother. "I mean, where I went."

"A peaceful valley," she said as she smiled. "With someone on the mountain looking out for everyone down below."

A day or so after Brad had regained consciousness, the nurses placed a young girl into the other hospital bed in Brad's room. Everyone, including her parents, seemed to know that the little girl was dying.

"Tell them how beautiful it is in heaven," a sister told Brad. "We know that you've been there. Tell them what their little Mary will soon see. Tell them that she will soon be with the angels and with Jesus."

Brad's first testimony regarding the afterlife, the survival of the soul, and the existence of ministering angelic beings was delivered in a hospital room in a Roman Catholic hospital in Des Moines, Iowa, in August 1947. And it was given to help two loving parents deal with the grief of surrendering their dying daughter into the hands of the angels.

From the perspective of his now fifty-eight years, Brad can see that his experience of near death at the age of eleven was a most fortuitous one.

Certainly one of the big questions that every thinking man and woman eventually asks is "Is there something within us that survives physical death?" Brad was fortunate to have had that eternal puzzler answered for him in the affirmative before he entered his teens.

Brad found out that there is an essential element within everyone, perhaps most commonly referred to as the soul, that does survive physical death, and that there are benevolent beings who care for us and who serve as our guardians and our guides. This knowledge shaped his attitude toward life.

WHAT BRAD HAD EXPERIENCED was a twofold phenomenon that has occurred in the lives of thousands of people: He was provided with his own personal proof of life after death, and his contact with angelic beings had been established.

Throughout his childhood and teenage years, Brad benefited from the intercession of a guardian angel on numerous occasions. Most often he heard an androgynous voice warning him to avoid situations that in every instance did prove to be dangerous for those who did not have the advantage of an angel's words of caution. And as has been stated, it was an angel's intercession that brought Sherry to him to be his true life partner.

Another phenomenon that Brad experienced is that hauntingly beautiful angelic manifestation known as celestial music. Numerous individuals who have undergone a near-death experience have heard the remarkably lovely sounds of an angelic chorus, but many others have delighted in the wondrous music without having undergone an NDE.

The Beautiful Phenomenon of Heavenly Music

A few months after his near-death experience, Brad was back on the farm in Iowa, walking through a grove of tall pine trees. As he sat down to rest and leaned back against the rusted wagon wheel of a long-discarded piece of farm machinery, he suddenly heard the strains of beautiful music.

For just a moment he thought that it might be the lulling moan of the wind through the pine boughs, but the eleven-year-old boy, who played the saxophone and who had always loved classical music, soon determined that the harmonious strains he heard were very much more symphonic and orchestral than the natural hums and sighs of nature.

When Brad heard the first chorus of heavenly voices rise to meet the orchestral accompaniment, he was convinced that the angels had returned to take him home. They had reconsidered their decision to allow him to return to his Earthwalk. It was, after all, his time to go.

While the boy searched the majestic clouds that floated across the brilliant blue Iowa sky for signs of descending angels, the symphonic music and the accompanying chorus of magnificent voices slowly began to fade away, leaving, at last, a puzzled farm boy wondering just exactly what it was that he had heard.

It wasn't long before Brad was reading about "ethereal" and "celestial" music in the books that he had convinced his grandmother Dina, the town librarian, to order for him. He soon learned that he was not unique in having heard the awesome and inspirational sounds of music from an invisible orchestra and chorus. And today, in the course of his research into the world of the mystical and the miraculous, he has spoken to numerous men and women, who, just as he, have been blessed with hearing the angelic music throughout the course of their lives.

Sing a Heavenly Hymn of Praise and Joy!

Shortly after nine-year-old Michael Solano had encountered an angel while he was walking in a beautiful wooded area near his home outside Saratoga Springs, New York, in the spring of 1948, he broke out in "an incredible heavenly song."

"The notes just seemed to pour out of my throat," he tried to explain to us. "I was able to move freely from octave to octave, to hit high notes beyond my imagining. Now, please understand that I had had no formal voice training of any kind whatsoever."

Michael's parents, both devout Roman Catholics, were mightily impressed with his angelically inspired vocal gifts. "I think they thought they suddenly had a one-boy Vienna Boys' Choir in their midst. Our priest thought I was singing church music from centuries back, and Sister Mary Margaret said that my singing cured her bad sinus headache."

The wonderful and mysterious outpouring of heavenly song left Michael after a few days, but he found that he had retained the remarkable ability to release individual musical "notes" at various tones and frequencies that appeared to affect dramatic healings in those who heard them.

"I have somehow retained this ability all my life," he said. "Although it may seem an unusual attribute for a real estate salesman, I am always willing to practice my unique style of healing ministry for any who will ask it of me."

Michael noted that Beethoven had once said that music is the mediator between the spiritual and the physical life. "I am thankful that I was given such a spiritual gift as a child. Music truly is the medicine of the soul."

Ashley's Celestial Music Box

Our friend Shirley Hessel wrote to us with an account of what she believed to be the manifestation of celestial music that indicated the presence of an angel watching over her granddaughter.

Her son told her that he and his wife would frequently awaken in the middle of the night to hear music coming from somewhere in their house. The music was unlike anything they had heard. "Angel music" was the closest description that he could manage in attempting to describe the sounds to Shirley.

On one particular night when the music awakened the couple, they were determined to track down the source of the "angel music." The young couple went from room to room until they realized at last that the music was clearly issuing from the bedroom of their two-year-old baby daughter, Ashley.

Once they were in her bedroom, they thought that the sounds might be coming from a music box. They picked up all the music boxes that little Ashley had in her room, but not one of them was playing. And though they knew very well that the glorious refrains that they had been hearing were far different from any of the familiar nursery tunes and Walt Disney melodies contained in Ashley's music boxes, they had felt compelled to be certain.

Although the young parents felt pride in the fact that their daughter seemed unusually bright (at just two years old she knew all the letters of the alphabet), they could determine no other meaning of the heavenly music than that the sounds of the celestial music box were a wonderful sign that an angel was watching over their precious little one.

STRUCTURING A PATTERN PROFILE
OF THE NEAR-DEATH EXPERIENCE

In comparing the results of our NDE research with those of the late Ian Currie, a lecturer at the University of Toronto, we arrived at a kind of synthesis of various aspects of the near-death experience as they have been described by hundreds of children who had survived an out-of-body journey and returned to life on Earth after knocking at heaven's door.

Here is what people have experienced:

- Seeing one's physical body apart from one's spiritual body
- A soaring sensation, a definite out-of-body movement
- Experiencing disorientation and confusion as to what is happening to them when they are ignored by doctors, nurses, loved ones, and other living persons
- The sensation of moving down a tunnel
- Perceiving a bright light
- Encountering an angelic being
- Discovering that their consciousness is free of the formerly accepted confines of time and space
- Being met by deceased relatives or friends, very often in the company of angels
- Having an angelic entity show them certain aspects of their earth lives, as if in review
- Receiving glimpses of a paradiselike existence and perhaps communicating with angels or deceased friends or relatives
- Finding that they are extremely reluctant to leave this beautiful state of existence and return to their physical bodies

A FAMOUS DOCTOR LEARNS
OF ANGELS AND THE AFTERLIFE

Our highly respected friend Dr. Elisabeth Kübler-Ross, a Swiss-born psychiatrist, commented some years ago that the more she went into after-death research, the more some scientific people wanted to tear her to pieces. "But I already have more than enough evidence that there is an afterlife," she said.

Since the early 1960s, when she began researching the claims of spiritual adventures from patients who had survived near-death experiences, Dr. Kübler-Ross has herself traveled out of the body, encountered angels, and received visits from materializations of former patients.

Sherry was privileged to have had Dr. Kübler-Ross as a professor in graduate school in Chicago in the 1960s, just prior to and after her book *On Death and Dying* was published.

"Elisabeth used to think that guardian angels were simply nice little stories we made up for children to keep them quiet," Sherry recalled. "She wasn't a particularly religious person before she began concentrating on her work with dying patients in the early sixties."

Dr. Kübler-Ross began noticing several common occurrences among her patients when they were on their deathbeds. They spoke to people, unseen by others, who very often were loved ones who had preceded them in death. At the clinical moment of death, most patients seemed immersed in an experience that left a telltale look of incredible peace on their faces.

Some of Dr. Kübler-Ross's patients, whose clinical functions had ceased but were eventually revived, shared experiences that could not have been possible without a transcendent spirit that survives death.

Dr. Kübler-Ross told Sherry how she became convinced beyond a shadow of a doubt that the soul transcends death. One of her dying patients, a twelve-year-old girl whose vital signs had completely ceased, revived and proceeded to tell her what she had experienced "on the other side."

The little girl told Dr. Kübler-Ross that she had been met by her older brother, whom she had described in detail and in terms that made him seem like an angel.

But, Kübler-Ross explained to Sherry, the little girl had never known her brother. He had died three months before she was born—and her parents had never even told her that she had had a brother!

Angels Sent Her Back
from the Garden of Lovely Flowers

When fifty-three-year-old Carmen Campabello of Lawton, Oklahoma, was a girl of ten, she lay seriously ill with diphtheria. She was so ill that, she learned later, her parents and her physician had resigned themselves to her imminent death.

One night she was lying in her bed, looking at the ceiling, when she suddenly found herself floating up through the darkness until she "saw some light and...a beautiful garden."

In the garden filled with lovely flowers she could hear soft music and laughter, and she was suddenly watching dozens of happy, shouting children at play.

When little Carmen tried to join them and sit with them at a drawing table, two gentle women appeared on either side of her.

"We are not ready for you yet," one of them said to her.

The two women led Carmen back the way she had come, and then the girl felt herself "falling through darkness...down and down."

"I know it was not a dream," Carmen says today. "I know that I stepped over the threshold of life and death, and that I met two angels and was shown what the afterlife holds for us."

Carmen added that she would always retain the mental image of heaven as a beautiful garden filled with lovely flowers. "I like to think that every soul in heaven is a flower in God's garden," she said.

C H A P T E R   5

Angelic Miracle Workers

A Life-Saving Baby's Formula from an Angel

HEN CRAIG GREEN OF BINGHAMTON, NEW YORK, was six months old, he was slowly dying because he could not retain any food. Because of some malady, which the doctors in 1933 were unable to diagnose, he weighed less than he had at birth.

Although the Green family physician and other medical experts had spent long hours with the infant, they were unable to determine either the cause or the remedy for baby Craig's rapidly deteriorating condition.

One night Sarah Green, Craig's sorrowing mother, looked toward a window in the bedroom and saw an angel robed in white coming through the screen.

"Be not afraid," the angel said in a gentle voice. "I have come to help you. Your baby is dying; but if you heed what I tell you, he will soon be well."

As the astonished mother listened, the supernatural visitor advised her to prepare the baby's formula according to his directions. "Make the formula of whole milk," the angel prescribed. "Add a little cream and beat an egg into the milk. Your baby will be able to keep this down."

The heavenly being walked to where the child lay sleeping. "Behold your son," the angel said, smiling. "He sleeps peacefully."

Tears coursed down Sarah's cheeks. "But the doctors say that little Craig will soon sleep in death," she said, barely managing to force the words past her sorrow.

The angel turned to her and spoke in a stern, authoritative manner: "Cease your weeping. You will make the formula as I have given it to you. Your boy will live to be a fine man.

"Now you will lie down," the angel seemed to add as a secondary command. "You will sleep long and peacefully. Good-bye."

Before the young mother's startled eyes, the angel floated through the screened window and disappeared.

When the doctor called the next day, Sarah decided not to tell him of her angelic visitation. But she did ask about the formula that the heavenly being had prescribed for her baby.

The doctor heard her out before he responded. "Well, under ordinary circumstances and conditions, I would feel that a change of diet might be harmful."

Before he completed his reply, the doctor hesitated several seconds. "But I must be honest with you, Mrs. Green. Little Craig seems to be walking the road to death. You might as well try the new formula. You have nothing to lose."

Since Craig Green is now sixty years old, there remains no question that the angel-prescribed formula worked for him.

"Mother told me how she knelt in prayer to God and thanked him for sending the angel to save her baby," Green told us.

"The change in formula might well have been the sole cause of my survival, but I have often felt that there was much more to the angel's visitation than that. I am convinced that the angel also exerted a great deal of healing energy and that the change in formula may have been only incidental to my rapid recovery."

Resigned to Dying,
Her Guardian Angel Appeared to Heal Her

Helen Hadsell of Dallas, Texas, who has written numerous inspirational works, told us that when she was sixteen years old, she was confined to bed for three months with rheumatic fever. At that time, medical science did not have a great deal to offer someone who had contracted this serious, and sometimes fatal, disease.

After three months of suffering and no improvement in her condition, the teenager overheard the doctor telling her mother that he could do very little more for her.

That night, Helen mustered up her courage and announced out loud to the universe that she was ready to die. She was tired of dragging out her pain. And if the doctor really couldn't do anything more for her...

"But someone had heard me announcing my resignation as Helen," she said. "As soon as I had made the demand to die, there appeared at my bedside a serene-looking young man. I was positive that he was not Jesus, but he did have a rather bright yellow glow around him. He reminded me of the holy pictures of the saints, which I was given by the nuns when I made good grades in school. He had such an air of peace and love radiating from him that I had no fear of his presence.

"'What makes you think that you're going to die, little girl?' he said. 'You have too much to live for and too much to do.'"

Helen knew that the angelic figure was real. And even though she understood his admonition, she was still determined to die. "What can I do tied to a bed for the rest of my life?" she asked.

The entity smiled and said, "You are healed. You will return to your studies. Later in life you will be inspired to write many experiences so that many will learn from you. This is the purpose for your life, and you will be guided."

When he had finished with his pronouncement, the angelic being seemed to fade away, as if disappearing into the wall.

Helen recalled that she was one excited teenage girl. "I yelled for my mother to come quickly. She took my temperature—and it was normal!

"She made me promise never to tell anyone about my 'visitor,' thinking it was only a strange dream. But the next morning my feet touched the floor for the first time in three months. Within a week I joined my family at the dinner table, and the following week I was back in school."

Mary Jobson's Angel Voices

It is always interesting to review historical cases of angelic interaction with children and compare and contrast them with their more contemporary counterparts. The following classic account remains controversial in that the invisible voice claiming to be that of an angel seemingly possessed its young host. At the same time, there have been few more remarkable episodes of claimed angelic interaction than in the incredible case of Mary Jobson.

It was between her twelfth and thirteenth year, in November 1839, when a young English girl named Mary Jobson began to suffer from a mysterious illness that afflicted her frail body for nearly eleven weeks. Throughout most of this period, the girl was attended by an invisible entity that spoke to many visitors in a "heavenly" voice.

A number of unusual phenomena added to the concern of Mr. and Mrs. Jobson as they ministered to their sick daughter. At first they were puzzled to hear the sound of rapping coming from the area of Mary's bed. Initially, they thought the child pounded at the bedstead while in the delirium of her fever, but on several occasions they were in the room and heard the knocking while Mary's hands were plainly in view.

Soon after the mysterious knockings began, a strange, whispering voice that seemed to come from nowhere in particular began to predict events in the Jobson family circle, which later occurred.

The Jobsons were no sooner accustomed to the manifestation of the whispering voice, when they were treated to drops of holy water that seemed to fall from the celling. To add to their appreciation of the remarkable blessing, an invisible organ began to play sweet and ethereal melodies.

The celestial music that attended the self-proclaimed angelic visitor is a most intriguing aspect of the mystery of Mary Jobson. Not only did numerous witnesses attest to having heard the melodious sound of an organ fill the room with strains of hymns, but on many occasions lovely voices of an invisible choir sang to its accompaniment.

At the onset of the angelic attachment to the sickly child, the Jobson family doctor exercised his skepticism, as did John Jobson, Mary's father; but the manifestations, especially the "heavenly voice," began to attract wide attention in the area.

On one occasion, soon after the visitation had begun, the girl's cautious father demanded of the voice that more holy water be delivered, and he received a large quantity of water dumped at his feet. Still not satisfied, he called for more of the heavenly liquid—and another deluge was forthcoming. Again he called for additional quantities and again and again until he had commanded the appearance of the holy water a full twenty times—and Mary's bedroom was drenched.

The invisible speaker assured the Jobson family and their friends that it was a good spirit and that it had originated from the highest of sources. Furthermore, the angel announced, it had come to administer good advice to all those who came to hear it.

Mary's teacher, Elizabeth Gauntlett, was summoned to Mary's bedside by the angelic voice while she was doing housework in her own home.

"Elizabeth, one of your students is ill," the voice informed her. "Go and see her. I promise you that the visit will be beneficial for you as well."

Miss Gauntlett obeyed the voice, inquired as to the address of her pupil, and later testified that she had received "many marvelous signs" at the bedside of the young girl.

The angel revealed to the distraught parents that their Mary had been temporarily "possessed" by a spirit of goodness. The Jobsons were told that though their daughter appeared to suffer, she did not.

"Mary does not know where her body is," the voice said. "Her own spirit has left this body, and I have entered it." Mary Jobson's bedroom became a sort of shrine as the girl's frail young body became a "speaking trumpet" for the revelations of the angelic entity, the "good spirit."

Once when the room was crowded with witnesses, the voice bade them look up toward the ceiling: "Look up, and you shall see the sun and moon appear."

As the bewildered assemblage heeded the good spirit's wishes, they beheld a beautiful representation of the celestial orbs appearing in lively colors of yellow and orange.

John Jobson immediately set about removing the figures from the ceiling, but he soon learned that the angel had intended its artwork to be permanent. He put his brush away when he discovered that after several coats of whitewash the figures remained visible.

Perhaps the most astounding materialization by the alleged angelic being was that of a lamb with a snow-white fleece. Margaret Watson was among those witnesses who were stunned by the animal's sudden appearance in Mary Jobson's bedroom, and her account of the experience was circulated widely.

At last, the voice announced that Mary Jobson would be the recipient of a healing miracle that would be wrought on June twenty-second.

The doctor advised the concerned parents that in his opinion, the miracle could not come too soon. According to his studied medical diagnosis, Mary was as ill as ever, and if the strange, undefined disease continued this peculiar course, death would be imminent.

When the appointed day arrived, Mary's strength appeared to be rapidly diminishing. Her fever had risen, and the doctor was not optimistic about the girl's chances of seeing another day.

At five o'clock the spirit voice instructed Mrs. Jobson to lay out some clothes for Mary. Too dazed by grief and worry to refuse, the woman did as she had been told. After this simple task had been performed, the voice ordered everyone from Mary's bedroom with the exception of her two-year-old brother.

The Jobsons and their doctor spent an anxious fifteen minutes outside the door of Mary's room before they heard the voice of the angel cry out, "Come in!"

When they entered the bedroom, they saw Mary sitting, smiling, in a chair, completely dressed, bouncing her baby brother on her knee.

From that moment on, Mary seldom suffered from illness of any kind. She matured into a very well-educated and highly respected woman, and she never received another visit from the angel, the "good spirit."

Her Guardian Angel Showed Her
a Preview of Her Adult Life

Kathryn O'Toole of Wichita, Kansas, told us that she remembers always having a guardian angel in constant communication with her.

"The earliest memory that I have of her speaking to me was at my fifth birthday party," Kathryn said. "I was wearing a pretty new blue dress that I thought was absolutely the most beautiful dress in all the world, and I was behaving like a little snot to the other children.

"When I went into the bathroom to wash sticky cake and ice cream off my hands, my angel gave me a gentle scolding and told me how to behave in a more appropriate manner."

Kathryn was eleven when her grandfather died. "I couldn't understand why everyone was crying at the funeral. My angel had shown me that we go to heaven after death, and my grandpa had been very sick before he died. I just knew that he had to be happier now, but my parents and relatives were acting upset with me because they didn't think I was showing the proper amount of grief.

"At the funeral I saw his spirit in the company of my angel, and Grandpa mentally told me that I was right to think of death as being just a 'crossing over.' At the same time, he seemed to approve of the ceremony and all the goings-on. I felt very close to him that day in a way I never had before."

When Kathryn turned thirteen, her angel appeared to her and showed her a preview of all the major events of her life up to the age of thirty-seven.

"I wouldn't look after the age of thirty-seven," she admitted. "So many things didn't make any sense to me when my angel gave me the preview of coming attractions, but all the big events have occurred just as she predicted. Now I am thirty-seven, and I wish that I hadn't stopped her from showing me more!"

The Gangster Who Made a Deal
with an Angel to Heal His Daughter

This fascinating account of a gangster's deal with an angel on behalf of his injured daughter came to us by way of a feature writer for a newspaper in a major Florida city. The journalist's source for the story was Bill Jameson, a former army intelligence officer who had also served a stint on the New York City police force before becoming a private investigator in Florida.

Jameson said that the racketeer—we'll call him Jerry Nichols—had been one of the criminal kingpins in Florida and had run the parts of the state under his control with an iron hand. Jameson had been keeping tabs on the gangster since the old days in New York, when Nichols was working his way up the higher rungs of the mob ladder.

Then, strangely, the gangster seemed to drop out of sight. When Jameson next discovered him, he was in a legitimate business and was preaching the word of God on the side.

Stunned, the private detective pressed his old nemesis for details, and Nichols was delighted to tell him the remarkable story of his conversion.

"My twelve-year-old daughter, Jackie, got hit by a car when she was walking home from school," Nichols began. "She was rushed to the hospital with her skull badly crushed. My wife, Brenda, and I were sweating it out in the waiting room, when this young doc comes out looking like he's lost the coin toss and he's the one who has to give us the bad news about our daughter.

"Brenda leaned against me like she was going to faint, and I told the medic to drop the suspense and cut to the chase. My coarse, blunt manner had its usual irritating effect, so he became pretty cold and direct and he just came out and said that he and the other doctors could offer us no hope for Jackie's recovery."

Nichols's wife went to pieces and the doctors had to give her a sedative.

"I had one of my boys drive her home, and I gave him the number of one of Brenda's friends," Nichols said. "I told him to call the lady and ask her to come and sit with Brenda while I stayed at the hospital."

Nichols sat by his daughter's bedside for the rest of the day and all through the night, but his beloved little Jackie, the princess of his heart, did not open her eyes even for a moment.

The gangster did not leave the hospital until the sun was coming up. He was walking toward his car across the deserted parking lot, when there appeared before him an angel, glowing in brilliant white light.

"This supernatural being's aura was so bright, so white, it hurt my eyes, and I could not make out its features too distinctly," Nichols said. "But I knew it was an angel."

The tough racketeer dropped to his knees. "Look, it's been so long, I don't know if I remember how to pray," he began his plea. "I know that I'm just a wiseguy. I've got too many sins to confess, so I admit up front that I am not worthy to ask anything of you. But please, oh, please, do something to help my daughter, Jackie."

Nichols began to weep unashamedly, allowing the tears to flow unchecked over cheeks bristling with stubble.

"So I'm a bum," he continued after he regained control of his voice. "But my Jackie is young. She's good. She's just about to become a young woman. Don't take her away before she's had a chance to live."

The angel stood before him, silent, unmoving, expressionless.

"So that's it." Nichols nodded soberly, believing that he had suddenly received some insight into the angel's master plan. "You want me, don't you? You want my life in exchange for my kid's. Okay, you've got it. Take me. Now. This minute. I don't care. I'll do whatever you want. I'll do whatever you say to save my baby."

Almost immediately after he had uttered those words, the angel vanished.

Puzzled and uncertain of exactly what had transpired, Nichols walked slowly to his car and sat in the driver's seat for several minutes before he felt that he had regained his composure enough to drive home safely.

When he pulled into his driveway, he saw Brenda standing on their front porch with her friend, Gloria, and Bennie, one of his boys. It was apparent that she was in better control of herself and that she was about to leave for the hospital.

They embraced in the driveway, and Nichols mumbled, "No improvement, babe. You go on back to sit with Jackie. I'll try to catch some winks."

A few hours later, Nichols was awakened by the ringing of the telephone at his bedside. It was Brenda calling from Jackie's hospital room.

"Sweetheart," she managed to say through her tears of joy, "our baby just opened her eyes and smiled at me!"

The doctors could not explain what had occurred to effect such a complete reversal of young Jackie Nichols' critical condition. She made a remarkable, miraculous recovery, and in a few days was discharged from the hospital to convalesce at home.

On the night after Jackie was discharged, Nichols had another visit from the angel while he was going over some account books in his study.

"Okay," he said, shrugging when the brilliantly glowing entity materialized before him. "It's payback time, right? Well, I always keep my word, so take my soul or whatever it is you want. A deal is a deal."

For the first time, Nichols was clearly able to perceive the supernatural being's eyes, and he felt himself being drawn into their incredible depths.

Jerry Nichols burst into a loud spasm of uncontrollable laughter. *"That's* what you want? You want me to quit the rackets? Then you might as well take my soul now, 'cause I'll soon be dead if I try to quit."

He stopped laughing as the angel's eyes exerted their full power.

Brenda was stunned when he told her that he had made the decision to quit the rackets. "This is too much joy," she said, beaming. "My daughter's life is spared and my husband is going legit. I am going to get drunk on happiness if I'm not careful!"

A WEEK LATER, WHEN THREE MEN came to call on him, Nichols could see they did not share Brenda's happiness over his decision. He recognized each one of them. They had been close "business associates" of his.

"You heard right, boys," Nichols replied to their direct questions. "I'm quitting the rackets and becoming a minister."

"They were very polite," Nichols recalled, "but I knew that they were very upset with me. When they asked me to come with them, I knew that they planned to kill me. I asked them please not to do it in front of the house where Brenda and Jackie could see it. They promised me that they would not."

Nichols drove with the mobsters some distance into the country. He had made up his mind that he would not beg for his life. Maybe this was the way the angel had planned it all along. Maybe this was just another way of trading his life for Jackie's.

"But then I heard that angel's voice inside my head," Nichols said. "What he was saying was crazy, but I knew that I had nothing to lose by repeating what he was telling me to say."

Nichols informed them that he had a quarter of a million dollars in the vault of "Mr. Big," Florida's mob boss. He explained that he did not want the money for himself or to bribe them, but he wanted the money to serve as an insurance policy for Brenda and Jackie.

"It had to be the power of the angel's words flowing through me," Nichols said, "for I managed to persuade them to take me to Mr. Big so that I might ask him to give the money to my family. I know it sounds unbelievable when you are talking about hardened tough guys, hit men, but somehow these men decided to take a chance and to go along with my dying request. It had to be a miracle, that's all there is to it.

"Mr. Big nearly went berserk with rage when he saw the three hoods walk into his office with me, the intended victim, in tow. He demanded to know why I wasn't dead."

Still taking heavenly dictation from the angel's voice inside his head, Nichols told the mob boss that he did not mind dying, but he wanted the money in Mr. Big's safe for his wife and daughter. The doomed man challenged the boss by reminding him that the money was, after all, truly his, not the mob's, because he had been the one who had collected it.

Once again Nichols knew that it had to be another miracle of angelic intervention that prevented the crime boss from having him killed on the spot; instead, Mr. Big asked him to explain why he had quit the rackets.

Nichols glanced upward, prayed for guidance, then told the boss and the three mobsters the full details of Jackie's terrible accident, the materialization of the angelic being, and the miraculous recovery of his daughter. Nichols also informed Mr. Big of his decision to become a minister in order to pay his debt to the angel.

"Mr. Big sat quietly for a long time in his massive leather chair, then he told the three hoods who had brought me to him to take me home," Nichols continued. "That was all there was to it. The angel had just performed another miracle.

"Mr. Big kept my quarter of a million, but I didn't want it anyway. I had all I wanted: my wife, my kid, and a chance to start a whole new life in service to the living God. Mr. Big was welcome to all the loot."

The money didn't do Mr. Big much good, Bill Jameson, the private detective, pointed out. The Florida mob boss was killed about ten months later in a gangland slaying.

Nichols, already an active lay preacher by that time, took his daughter to the cemetery where Mr. Big lay buried. He said a brief prayer over the mobster's headstone and told Jackie that the man had been an "old friend."

Nichols and his daughter left the cemetery tightly holding each other's hand.

CHAPTER 6

Angels: Our Ever-Present Comforters in Life and in Death

EVEREND HARRY CLARK WAS MINISTERING to a dying girl, when he saw an angel materialize beside the child's deathbed. As the heavenly being stood beside her, he heard the angel say, "I have come to take you home, Kristin."

"I was then further astonished to observe three other angels join the angel at the bedside of the eight-year-old girl," Reverend Clark said. "Kristin's parents seemed aware of a holy presence in the hospital room, but they apparently saw nothing. I could tell, however, by the widened eyes of their four-year-old son, that he was able to see the angels quite clearly."

Reverend Clark stated that he then saw a hazy white mist rise above the girl's body.

"This mist eventually congealed to take on a perfect replica of Kristin's physical body," he said. "After the soul essence had been released from its physical shell, the child's spirit left in the company of the angels. I felt that my life had been blessed and that my ministry had been enriched by my being permitted to observe the deliverance of a soul into the keeping of the heavenly messengers."

His Son's Soaring Spirit Clapped Its Hands for Joy

Paul Savastano of Overland Park, Kansas, saw what he believed to be the spirit of his twelve-year-old son, Adam, as it was disengaging itself from the physical body. The cloudlike vapor took on human shape, clapped its hands for joy, then passed upward through the ceiling in the company of an angel.

On Either Side of His Son's Body, He Beheld an Angel

Earl Dayley of Denver, Colorado, is certain that at the time of his ten-year-old son's death, he saw Bruce's spirit leaving the body as a luminous cloud and rise upward through the ceiling.

"On either side of my son's spirit body I saw an angel," Dayley said. "Both were clothed in white and emanated a brilliant light."

Roxana's Spirit Floated Toward the Window— and Her Guardian Angel

Margaret De Camarillo stated that as she entered her six-year-old daughter's hospital room, she saw a small oval light emerging from Roxana's head. It floated toward the window, where it was met by an angelic figure.

"Before I could reach my daughter, I knew that she was dead," Mrs. De Camarillo said. "I summoned a nurse, who quickly verified that my daughter had died."

She Saw Her Friend's Spirit Clothed in a White Angelic Robe

Janice Scott of Covington, Kentucky, said that in 1941, when she was only eight years old, she had a close friend named Charlotte, who became suddenly ill while they were playing house in Charlotte's room and who died before a doctor could arrive.

"Immediately after Charlotte's heart stopped beating," Janice said, "I saw a mistlike steam take on a human shape and become well formed and well defined. It was the image of Charlotte, clothed in a pearly white, cloudlike robe. It was the face of my dear friend, but glorified, without any visible trace of the spasm of pain that had so suddenly seized her and contorted her features before her death."

ANGELS WHO MINISTER AT DEATHBEDS

In his ongoing research of several years, Reverend W. Bennett Palmer found that accounts in which the dying have been seen leaving their bodies bear a remarkable resemblance to each other whether they are ancient or modern, whether they originate from primitive tribes or from the most sophisticated civilizations.

In the typical account, a deathbed witness sees a mist or a cloudlike vapor emerging from the mouth or head of the dying person. The vaporous substance may then take on a human form, which is generally a duplicate of the living person—only in many cases any deformities or injuries are partially or wholly absent. Angels are seen standing ready to accompany the newly freed spirit form, and spirits of the deceased's previously departed loved ones are also often reported in the company of attending angels.

In several reports, the immediate process of death is not witnessed, but the deceased is seen leaving the earth, most often accompanied by angels. Frequently, such spirit and angel leave-taking is seen in the sky, but to many researchers this seems to be a symbolic mode of disappearance rather than an indication that heaven is in any particular area of space.

A Beautiful Lady in White
Took the Child's Spirit from the Nursery

Dr. Marshall Oliver was visiting a sick child who had been slowly dying because of complications from pneumonia.

"As I turned to pick up my medical bag, I saw a beautiful 'lady' dressed in white approaching the child's crib," he said. "I knew that I was not observing any member of that or any other earthly family.

"The lovely being bent over the crib, and I saw a mistlike substance begin to flow from the child's mouth. The mist seemed to collect in a kind of puddle above the child until it grew more definite in shape and became an exact counterpart of the infant. The beautiful entity in white then took the spirit form of the child into its arms—and passed right through the wall of the nursery with the child cradled next to her breast.

"When at last I recovered my mental equilibrium, I examined the child and found that it had died at that moment."

An "Earth-Angel" Receives Her Heavenly Crown

Dr. David Cardoni of Brooklyn, New York, said that while he was attending the funeral of a dear friend's thirteen-year-old daughter, he perceived the vaporlike image of the girl hovering near the casket. There was no question in his mind that Anne Marie was truly clinically dead before the funeral, but he had once heard it stated that on some occasions the soul may linger for a time to ease the sorrow of the surviving loved ones.

"I knew that Anne Marie's brief life had been one of kindness and service to others," Dr. Cardoni said. "The girl had been a sincere, practicing Christian, a true angel on Earth."

But the physician was startled when he perceived a group of white-robed children, or cherubs, appear with chaplets of flowers that appeared as though they had been "woven of mingled sunbeams and roses." Also assembled near the coffin were white-robed spirits, whom he recognized as deceased relatives of Anne Marie's family.

"As the funeral service progressed, I saw a beautiful angel robed in the purest white approach the spirit of Anne Marie," Dr. Cardoni said. "In its hands the angel bore a lovely wreath, the center of which supported a large white rose. With this floral diadem the angel crowned the spirit of Anne Marie, and the image of the girl, together with the attending angels and the white-robed spirits of her loved ones, appeared to float away, upward, toward the ceiling."

Little Gina Was Sprinkled with "Angels' Tears"

Lorene Decesare of Escondido, California, said that beginning on August 19, 1978, and continuing until her daughter's death on November 21, the four-year-old girl would be sprinkled by water from some unknown source.

"This occurred daily, at eight o'clock each evening," Mrs. Decesare said. "At that time, each day, our little Gina would be blessed by the angels."

Because there appeared to be no possible "natural" explanation and because the phenomenon seemed to be somehow connected with their daughter's coming death, Mrs. Decesare and her family called the mysterious droplets of water "angels' tears."

According to Mrs. Decesare, various individuals witnessed the phenomenon of the falling water drops and were able to hear their slow, rainlike patter. The "angels' tears" fell on little Gina wherever she might happen to be at eight o'clock in the evening. The drops also splattered on anything she might be holding or that might be near her at the time.

The manifestation of the tears ceased when four-year-old Gina Decesare left with the angels on November 21, 1978, at eight o'clock in the evening.

Sheri Saw the Angels Take Her Mother and Her Sister

Gilbert Axton's wife, Ethel, and his nine-year-old daughter, Maribel, were killed in an automobile accident in Bloomington, Indiana, and his six-year-old daughter, Sheri, was severely injured.

"In my deep sorrow, I had no idea of how I was going to break the news to Sheri that her mother and her sister were dead," Axton said. "I stood outside her hospital room for several minutes, praying for guidance. I asked also for the strength to go on with our life together, for now it would be just the two of us."

Steeling himself to the awful task at hand, Gilbert Axton entered his daughter's hospital room, trying his best to fight back the tears that spilled down his cheeks.

But before he could break the news to Sheri, she told him that she already knew about the death of her mother and sister.

"While I was lying on the ground beside the car, I saw a beautiful angel come to get Mommy," she said. "The angel started to go back to the sky with Mommy, but then he stopped. He came back to the ground and stood over Maribel for a little bit, like he was trying to make up his mind. And then he took Maribel by the hand, too, and took both of them with him to heaven."

The "Pure Phenomenon" of a Child's Deathbed Vision

Among the most moving of all accounts of angelic interaction with children are those reports of angels who manifest to help dying boys and girls make their transition from life to death and beyond. Even the most resistant of skeptics must acknowledge the power of such deeply emotional experiences.

Professor Charles Richet, a well-known psychical researcher, was not an exponent of claims that a soul or spirit survives the body after physical death. Colleagues were well aware that Dr. Richet resisted the survival theory almost to the end of his own days on Earth. But the skeptical researcher found his rigid position softening when he began to investigate cases of the deathbed visions of children. In his opinion, such manifestations constituted the purest type of phenomenon in the vast realm of psychical research.

She Was Invited to Accompany
Her Son's Preview of Heaven Before His Death

Ginny Ebersole of Dayton, Ohio, saw angels in the sickroom of her son, Allen, twelve hours before his death.

"I had been praying for his recovery," she said, "but when I saw the angels, I knew that they had come to call him home."

Mrs. Ebersole went on to describe a most extraordinary experience that she shared with her son before his final passing.

"When I first saw the two angels appear in Allen's sickroom, I cried out in tears that I would not let them take him away from me," she said. "One of them turned to me and smiled and reached out his hand to me. I felt myself losing consciousness—and then I was walking with Allen in the spiritual realm."

It is Mrs. Ebersole's earnest belief that she was blessed with such a heavenly gift so that her grief in losing her son would be diminished. "I saw many angels, all of whom welcomed Allen to the spiritual realm with great and loving kindness. I beheld the heavenly kingdom and began to feel at peace in my own spirit."

Finally, one of the angels told her that she must return to her physical body. She could walk no farther with Allen into the lovely scenery and paradisical environment of the glorious heavenly domain.

"I embraced Allen and bade him farewell," she said. "In a blur of motion I was once again in my flesh form, lying across Allen's bed. My sister, Donna, who had maintained the vigil with me, told me that I had been in a kind of trance state for nearly twelve hours. During that time, she said, Allen had made his transition."

"Mommy, Two Angels Are in the Room with Us!"

Eleanor Carey of China Springs, Texas, stated that as her eleven-year-old daughter, Bonnie, lay dying, she suddenly opened her eyes and said, "Mommy, I can see two angels in the room. Can you see them?"

Mrs. Carey knelt at her daughter's side and embraced her, trying to hold back the tears of final parting. "You thought I was asleep, Mommy, but I wasn't. Two angels came into the room, and they have been talking to me of the most wonderful things."

Later, just as Bonnie's eyes began to close in death, an expression of delightful surprise came over her face.

"It was as though she had seen something glorious to behold," Mrs. Carey said. "Something glorious beyond all conception. That look of inexpressible delight remained on her face after death."

"Ginger Makes Such a Beautiful Angel"

As eleven-year-old Gary Laker lay on his deathbed in Moline, Illinois, he began to speak of seeing angels approaching him, as if from a distance. As his parents sensed the end was near, they began to weep and to clutch each other for support. The Lakers' pastor, Reverend Schelle, bent over the boy and whispered, "Gary, when the angels come for you, let us know."

In a short while, Gary asked for his parents and Pastor Schelle to come near. "The angels are here with me now," be said in a voice suddenly so much stronger than a few moments before. "They're robed in white, but they don't seem to have any wings. They look just like people...beautiful people."

A few minutes later, Gary added, "Grandpa Laker is coming for me. And there's Aunt Joan. They're walking toward me with the angels."

Mrs. Laker pressed her forehead to her husband's chest and wept freely into her handkerchief. Gary was naming deceased loved ones who were apparently joining the angels to take his spirit home to heaven.

"And Mom...Dad! Ginger is here too. Oh, I'm not so afraid to leave you now with Ginger here too."

The Lakers exchanged puzzled glances. Ginger Reedy was Gary's favorite cousin. They were both the same age and seemed truly to enjoy each other. But Ginger was very much alive in Ann Arbor, Michigan.

Gary took a deep, shuddering breath, and then, just before he died, he said, "Tell Aunt Renee that Ginger makes a beautiful angel."

A few hours later, after they had taken care of painful necessary matters at the hospital, the Lakers returned to their home in the terrible state of loss and shock that accompanies the death of a cherished loved one. They were grateful that Pastor Schelle had accompanied them and had promised to stay with them awhile longer to help them through the first hours of bereavement.

When the telephone rang, Pastor Schelle indicated that he would answer it. "Don't worry," he said. "I'll explain matters to whoever is calling."

The clergyman's features were solemn and somewhat drawn when he reentered the room. As he stepped behind the couch to place comforting hands on the shoulders of the grieving couple, he informed them that friends from Ann Arbor had just called to notify them of the death of Mrs. Laker's niece, Ginger, who had been killed earlier that day in an automobile accident. The girl had died just three hours before her cousin Gary.

An Angel Clothed in Brilliant Light
Knocked on Their Door for Baby Denny

When Edna Carney was eleven years old, her parents adopted a baby boy, whom all the family loved very much.

"But right from the beginning, even I could see that Denny's skin had a waxen pallor to it," Edna said. "And I could see that both my parents and Dr. Gilmore were worried."

For a time, little Denny's health seemed to improve, and it appeared that the worst had passed.

"Then one night in November, just a couple of days before Thanksgiving in

1964, Mom and I were getting ready to go to bed, when we heard a loud knock at the front door," Edna said. "We were startled, because it was late at night, and Dad was working the late shift at the factory.

"We stood there, facing the door, not knowing what to do. And then we really got scared when we heard the door latch click—and we saw the door slowly swing open."

To their complete astonishment, Edna and her mother saw an angelic figure in shining white enter their home and close the door slowly behind it. Without a word, the being, who was bathed in brilliant light, crossed the room and went over to where baby Denny lay sleeping.

The angel reached out its arms as if to take the baby. Then it lowered its arms, faced the wide-eyed mother and daughter—and turned to walk away. Halfway to the door, the being disappeared.

"I was so frightened that my teeth were chattering," Edna recalled. "At last my mother broke the silence by asking me if the experience had been real and whether or not I had seen what she had seen. I answered her by saying that if she thought that she had seen an angel, then I had undergone the same experience she had. I added my opinion that the angel had wanted to take Denny with it."

At that moment, baby Denny began to moan and to toss restlessly in his crib. For nearly a week, three doctors sought to save the infant's life. Then, on a Sunday evening, the baby boy smiled...and died.

"Although no one saw the angel again," Edna said, "I will forever believe that it returned for my little brother. In my personal interpretation of the incident, the angel's initial visit had been for the purpose of preparing us for the tragic event that was soon to come. Thirty years after the visitation, I will testify that the appearance of the angel deepened our family's faith in God.

An Angel Manifested
to Sing of Comfort at Her Last Rites

Pastor T. A. Van Campen shared an account from Depression days when a poor family from Oklahoma suffered the additional sorrow of losing a young daughter. The family so desperately wanted a Christian burial service, but at that time clergymen were almost nonexistent in the area.

A friend of the family's volunteered to ride to a nearby village and do his best to convince some person of the cloth to accompany him back to where the mourners were waiting in an old deserted church.

The sun was moving low on the horizon, and neither the friend nor the preacher were in sight. The father and mother were brokenhearted, and the assembled mourners were becoming despondent.

Then a beautiful woman appeared outside the old church. No one saw where she came from and no one knew who she was. She opened the door and walked to the front of the church, where the child lay at rest in a crude wooden coffin. Standing near the girl's body, she began to sing a lovely hymn, rich with spiritual meaning and comfort.

When the stranger had completed the beautiful song of love and peace, she walked out the door of the church and disappeared. No one in that region ever saw her again, but the impression remained firm in the minds of the witnesses that they had perceived an angel, an angel of comfort who had manifested to help a young girl achieve her final earthly rest.

The "Little Girl" Came to Get Cindy

Armon Lundquist has often told the story of the time when he witnessed the manifestation of an angel who, he believes, appeared in the form of a beautiful young girl in order not to frighten the six-year-old child whose soul the angel had come to take home to heaven.

"It was back in 1948," he remembered. "I was still farming my family's home place in Missouri. One of the neighbors, Harvey Steinbruck, got himself in trouble by writing bad checks and was sent up for a stretch in the state penitentiary. I felt sorry for his wife and young daughter all alone out in the country, and I would stop by from time to time to look in on them and to chop wood for their cookstove and fireplace."

Armon saw the angel with his own eyes on that afternoon in early April. He had just finished chopping a bin full of firewood, and he cheerily walked up to Mrs. Steinbruck, who sat on the front porch swing, mending a pair of her daughter's socks.

"Well, Patty, I got your wood bin loaded as high as it will go. You'll be able to keep out any spring chill," he said. He knew that Cindy had been ill most of the winter and that she still suffered from a persistent cough. It would be important to Patty to be able to have a fire in the house during the evening hours in order to keep Cindy warm.

Patty Steinbruck looked up from her sewing, a smile of gratitude on her face. "Thank you, Armon. I really don't know what I would do without folks as kindly as you. Please sit here a bit while I get you some coffee. I've got a fresh pot brewing on the stove."

"A Swede never turns down coffee," he said, grinning. "I would appreciate a cup before I head for home to start chores."

While Mrs. Steinbruck went inside to fetch the coffee, Lundquist's attention was directed to her daughter, who came suddenly around the corner of the house, walking at a brisk pace. Her eyes wide with excitement, the six-year-old girl began to speak to him, but her words were shattered by a harsh spasm of coughing.

"Oh, honey," Mrs. Steinbruck scolded gently as she returned with the cup of coffee for their neighborly benefactor. "You've been overdoing again. You mustn't run or get so excited. What's wrong?"

"I was only going to tell Mr. Lundquist that my friend came back again to see me," Cindy said after her mother had wiped her mouth with a handkerchief. "She is so pretty. Do you know her, Mr. Lundquist?"

"Who's that?" Lundquist asked, more out of politeness than genuine curiosity. He could think of no other young girls in the neighborhood.

"Oh, Cindy has been making believe that she has a playmate," Mrs. Steinbruck said before her daughter could respond. "It gets lonely out here, of course, but she can be so silly. And she has a wild imagination, that's for sure. She keeps talking about this beautiful young girl who comes to see her. It's all in her head."

Cindy's lower lip quivered in an amusing blend of pout and determination. She walked around the corner of the house in the direction from which she had so recently emerged, and the two adults on the porch heard her triumphant cry. "She's still there! Come and see! Come and see!"

Lundquist and Patty Steinbruck joined Cindy and followed the direction indicated by her pointing finger.

"We were amazed to behold a radiant young girl standing in the gateway of the Steinbrucks' backyard," Lundquist said. "She was ten or eleven years old, I would guess; and she was possessed of a rare, unearthly beauty. When the strange little girl realized that all of us could see her, her lips parted in a lovely smile. She held out her arms to Cindy, who began to walk toward her."

Mrs. Steinbruck reached out to clutch her daughter's hand. "No, Cindy," she cried, her voice filled with fear. "Stay here by Mommy!"

Cindy's small face screwed into an expression of disappointment, and she twisted her little body in an effort to shake off her mother's possessive fingers. "But I want to go with the pretty girl," she sobbed.

Mrs. Steinbruck shook her head violently. "No...no! She's too pretty. She's too perfect to be real. She's not of this world."

Then, turning to Lundquist, she cried, "Oh, my God, Armon! What *is* she?"

As Lundquist recalled the encounter, he was unable to take his eyes off the ethereal girl in the gateway. The more he stared at her, the more he became convinced that she was a visitor from the unseen world.

"Beauty that great could be possessed only by an angel," he finally answered. "I think she must be an angel."

Lundquist said that he glanced quickly at Cindy. She had stopped crying, and now stood perfectly still between them. She smiled at the beautiful stranger, appearing as if her entire being wished only to run to her outstretched arms.

"In that one quick glance toward Cindy, I was shocked and dismayed to discover that the mysterious figure had vanished," Lundquist said. "I told Patty that I was now completely convinced that we had been gazing upon an angel, for no human being could have disappeared so quickly."

Just to be certain, Lundquist walked to the gate and looked around, but the whole countryside was open farmland. There were no trees, bushes, or shrubs behind which the girl could have run and hidden.

Lundquist returned to the front porch with what he remembers as a growing sense of foreboding.

He looked at little Cindy, who had once again begun to cough in all the excitement of the appearing and disappearing angelic figure. He knew that she had always been a quiet, well-behaved child, but very frail and sickly. When Harvey Steinbruck had been sent to the penitentiary and all the neighbors had pledged to help the small family whenever they could, Lundquist remembered that wise old Mrs. Thorenson, who had brought up ten children of her own, had said that poor little Cindy was "not long for this world."

When Patty Steinbruck broke her own silence, Lundquist was startled to hear that she harbored similar thoughts concerning the fate of her daughter.

"I can't help worrying about Cindy," she told him after her daughter had gone into the house to get a drink of water. "I think what we saw means that Cindy is going to die real soon. I'm convinced of it."

Nine days later, Lundquist was grieved to hear that little Cindy Steinbruck had died. He had become caught up in the spring fieldwork, and he had not returned to the Steinbruck place since that incredible afternoon when the angel had appeared.

When Lundquist and his wife came to pay their respects at the funeral home, the grieving Mrs. Steinbruck drew him aside.

"Cindy went into a coma, and she never came out of it," she told him. "But do you know what she said just before she slipped into unconsciousness? She said, 'Mommy, that beautiful little girl has come again. This time I am going to go with her.'"

Lundquist reached out to take Mrs. Steinbruck's hand in a gentle clasp of loving friendship and in unspoken recognition of the remarkable knowledge that they had shared of the unseen world.

"Both of us knew then for certain that we had been privileged to see the beautiful angel that had been sent from heaven to reclaim little Cindy's soul," he said. "Later, when I discussed all of this with Pastor Jacobsen, he said that it was likely that an angel had taken the shape of a little girl so as not to frighten Cindy and to make her transition to heaven just that much easier."

Three Beautiful Angels Appeared at His Daughter's Deathbed

Harry Gunderson of Duluth, Minnesota, described the following angelic visitation that occurred at his fifteen-year-old daughter's deathbed.

"Megan's mother had just left the hospital room to get some much-needed rest. The doctors had told us that the end was very near for our daughter, and they allowed us to lie down and get whatever sleep we could in an empty room down the corridor.

"I had begun to read the Bible for solace, when I looked up to see three separate clouds of mist float through the closed window and into the hospital room. I became completely enraptured by the manifestation, unable to speak or to move. As I watched, the clouds enveloped Megan's bed.

"As I gazed through the mist, I saw a woman's form take shape. It was transparent and had a golden sheen. It was a figure so glorious in appearance that no words can adequately describe it.

"The beautiful entity was dressed in a long, Grecian-type robe, and there was a brilliant tiara on her head. The angel—for I knew it had to be an angel— remained motionless with its hands uplifted over the form of Megan, seemingly engaged in prayer. Then I noticed two other beautiful angels kneeling by our daughter's bedside.

"In a few minutes there appeared lying horizontally above Megan's physical body a form that I can describe only as her spirit duplicate. It seemed at first to be connected to her material body by a thin golden cord.

"The whole experience lasted for about two hours, and in all that time I was literally unable to blink an eye. And since it was very late at night, there were no intrusions by hospital personnel.

"I so wish that I had somehow been able to stir myself from the trancelike state and summon my wife to behold the beautiful angelic manifestation occurring around the bedside of our dying daughter. As soon as our beloved Megan had taken her last breath, the three angels and the spirit duplicate vanished."

FOR OF SUCH IS THE KINGDOM OF HEAVEN— WHY ANGELS LOVE AND CARE FOR CHILDREN

When certain disciples became unnecessarily protective of their teacher's time by shooing away the small children who clustered about him, Jesus admonished them, "Suffer the little children to come unto me, and forbid them not, for of such is the kingdom of God."

Knowing how Jesus felt about the little ones, we cannot truly wonder when we find story after story of angelic figures assuming an active and often protective role in the lives of children. Indeed, it seems as though access to heaven and heavenly beings is much more easily affected in the wonder years of childhood before the demands of societal adjustment have begun to blunt the natural inclination to perceive the sacred all around us.

In his poem "On the Death of a Friend's Child," James Russell Lowell says that "Children are God's apostles, sent forth, day by day, to preach of love and hope and peace."

In *The Brothers Karamazov*, the great Russian novelist Fyodor Dostoyevsky has one of his characters advising us to "Love children especially, for like the angels they too are sinless, and they live to soften and to purify our hearts, and, as it were, to guide us."

Mary Howitt, the nineteenth-century English author, agrees that our children have been sent to us by God for a far greater purpose than merely to keep up the race: "Children enlarge our hearts and make us unselfish and full of kindly sympathies and affections. Children give our souls higher aims....My soul blesses the great Father every day that he has gladdened the Earth with little children."

BUT IT IS NOT ONLY BECAUSE children are innocent and vulnerable or that they enlarge the hearts of those around them that they are so loved and cared for by the angels. It seems certain that the benevolent beings fully understand that there can be no transformation of the often unkempt garden that is the planet

Earth unless the seedlings, the children, are carefully nurtured and taught which paths lead to darkness and the noxious weeds of self-destruction and which lead to sunlight and the opportunities for spiritual growth.

Our children are far more than our present pride and joy or "instruments to keep us full of kindly sympathies," they are our most sincere expression of hope that there will be a tomorrow for the human species. The efforts we extend on behalf of our children constitute the investment that we make in the future of all humankind.

The old-time evangelist Billy Sunday was not far off the mark when he said that the only way on God's earth that we will ever make our world a better place is by getting hold of the children and seeing to it that they are set on the path of spiritual awareness. "You get boys and girls started right," Sunday advised, "and the Devil will have to hang crepe on his door and close up shop."

IT SEEMS THAT THE ANGELS fully realize that each child born into the world offers a second chance for all humanity.

As the author Kate Douglas Wiggin expressed it: "Every child born into the world is a new thought of God, an ever-fresh and radiant possibility."

The angels have as their mission the solemn duty to guide and to guard the children of Earth so that the dwellers on our planet may truly receive a second chance to explore all the radiant possibilities of our heavenly heritage.

Angels Around
The World

Angels Around The World

BRAD STEIGER
SHERRY HANSEN STEIGER

Guideposts®

CARMEL • NEW YORK 10512

This Guideposts edition is published by special arrangement with
Fawcett Columbine/Ballantine Books.

Copyright © 1996 by Brad Steiger and Sherry Hansen Steiger

All rights reserved under International and Pan-American
Copyright Conventions.

http://www.guideposts.org

Library of Congress Catalog Card Number: 96-96530

ISBN: 0-449-98369-2

Cover and book design by José R. Fonfrias
Typeset by Composition Technologies, Inc.
Manufactured in the United States of America

Millions of angels walk the earth unseen,
both when we sleep and when we wake.
JOHN MILTON

Contents

Contents

Missouri

New Jersey

New Mexico

~ *Introduction* ~

ANGELS—THE COMMON LINK BETWEEN HUMANS AND GOD IN ALL CULTURES

There are two angels, that attend unseen
Each one of us, and in great books record
Our good and evil deeds. He who writes down
The good ones, after each action closes
His volume, and ascends with it to God.
The other keeps his dreadful day-book open
Till sunset, that we may repent; which doing,
The record of the action fades away,
And leaves a line of white across the page.

—HENRY WADSWORTH LONGFELLOW, *"The Golden Legend"*

THROUGHOUT THE COURSE OF HUMAN HISTORY, communication and guidance from God has been delivered by angels in a variety of ways to multitudes all over planet Earth. Regardless of religion, color, or creed, every human culture has been granted the heavenly gift of angelic intervention.

From the very act of creation and the origins of humankind, angels have served as the cosmic link between humans and God.

There are many names for the angels. The word for *angel* in Sanskrit is *angiras*; in Hebrew, *malakh*, meaning "messenger," or *bene elohim*, for "God's children"; and in Greek, *Hoi Hagioi*, the "Holy Ones." In Arabic, the *malakah* are the celestial beings; in Italian, the *putti* are cherubs; and in India, multiwinged angels or beings are called *Garudas*.

The Bible refers to angels as Sons of God, Mediators, and Holy Watchers. In general, their main purpose seems to be to make humans better people. To accomplish this, they advise, rescue, warn, punish, and instruct. They sing and make celestial music, on occasion heralding their approach with trumpets. They are able to speak in many tongues, and whatever their utterances, they make them with power and authority. They can be heard by one or by many— sometimes only as the "still, small voice within." The Bible also states that the angels were made a little higher than humans, yet it depicts some angels as sitting at the feet of God.

Angelic beings may appear in dreams by night or in visions by day. They can be visible or invisible. They can be felt as a presence, or can appear as a mist, a haze, a cloud, a pillar of cloud, a pillar of fire, or a burning bush. They can fill a room with light or manifest as a blinding light, a ball of light, or a Light Being. They can come and go in chariots and ride on the wind. They can appear and disappear in the blink of an eye. And sometimes they can even be mistaken for ordinary human beings, acting human enough to knock on a door, dine at a table, or lodge as an overnight guest.

Angels have delivered a people or a nation—but they have also destroyed cities and annihilated entire armies. They have sheltered, rescued, and healed many human supplicants—but they have also directed pestilence and other terrible afflictions.

In all of the world religions, angels seemed most concerned with calling upon all people to examine their souls, to improve their treatment of their fellow beings, to resist passing judgment on others, and to put aside intolerance and prejudice in favor of becoming more loving and forgiving.

St. Thomas Aquinas said, "An angel can illumine the thought and mind of man by strengthening the power of vision, and by bringing within his reach some truth which the angel himself contemplates." Within the last decade, angels have once again become recognized by large numbers of ordinary people as our heavenly guides and benefactors. Some theorize this recent angelic activation is due to the approaching millennium. Others suggest that our celestial guardians have become greatly concerned about environmental abuse of the planet. Still others warn that Judgment Day is at hand.

For whatever reasons, hundreds of people have come forward to declare that angels have given them warnings, admonitions, prophetic messages, visions, special assignments, and even physical assistance and financial aid. Thousands of sincere men and women have forthrightly stated their heartfelt belief that angels have provided them with guidance, protection, and assistance in the challenges that they face in life, and that angels have walked beside them through personal crises and times of testing.

MANY THOUGHTFUL SCHOLARS throughout the ages have observed that one of the basic purposes of angels in all forms of religious expression is to help humans understand that they are immortal, that their spirit comes from a divine world— a heavenly, angelic realm—and that it may also return to that higher dimension. And, of greatest importance now in our ever-shrinking world, all of the sacred teachings relayed by the angelic messengers teach respect and tolerance for other human beings.

In our research, counseling, lecturing, teaching—stories have been sent to us or told to us. In addition, in response to our questionnaire, people worldwide have sent us their stories. The stories contained in *Angels Around the World* will explore the many ways in which angelic beings manifest to all peoples and all cultures and religions. We pray that our efforts will enlighten you, illuminate your path more clearly, and enable you to distinguish a purpose and a plan in a seemingly chaotic world. We also hope that a pattern will emerge that will profoundly demonstrate that we are all loved by God and the angels.

OUR QUESTIONNAIRE BRINGS REPORTS OF ANGELS AROUND THE WORLD

In *Angels Over Their Shoulders*, we described the questionnaire of mystical and paranormal experiences that we have been sending to readers of our books for nearly thirty years. In addition to answering the survey questions, many men and women who have undergone angelic encounters feel compelled to share additional details of their interaction with heavenly beings.

Here are a few excerpts from those accounts of our readers telling us of angels in action around the world:

JORDAN

A woman we'll call Anna Hanke, an administrative assistant from Brooklyn, told of the time that she was riding in an open Jeep in Jordan in 1970. She was in the backseat on the left, and a nurse was on the right.

"We were going down a highway when a loud voice yelled at me in English: 'Move!'" Anna told us.

"I was so frightened by this booming voice that I immediately jumped to my left. At that instant a shot rang out, and the nurse was struck and killed. I would have been killed had the bullet hit me instead."

Anna asked the driver if he had yelled to her to move. "Of course not," he said. "I didn't even see the sniper!"

"I know that I have heard that voice before," Anna said. "It was my guardian angel warning me."

ISRAEL

David Rosenfeld wrote to tell of the extraordinary incident that occurred while he was serving in the Israel Defense Forces.

"It would have been a fatal accident while on maneuvers," he told us. "An accident, but nonetheless, I certainly would have been dead."

One of Rosenfeld's fellow soldiers, less than ten feet away from him, accidentily discharged his rifle.

"I was literally looking right down the barrel of that rifle. Somehow I knew that the rifle was going to fire."

And then everything went into slow motion.

"It was almost as if it were all happening on a strip of motion picture film and time was advancing frame by frame," he said. "I could see the bullet that was moving toward my head, and somehow, it was moving slowly enough for me to get out of the way."

In the next millisecond, a bright light moved between Rosenfeld and the bullet and pushed him away with a powerful shove.

"As I went sprawling to the ground, I saw that all the other soldiers were frozen into immobility. But as soon as my body struck the earth, everything resumed normal speed. That's when I heard the loud report of the rifle and the bullet as it ricocheted off a rock.

"I know that what I have told you is physically impossible, but if it had not happened just as I have said, I would not be around to tell you about it. I have always believed that I had a guardian angel, and I am certain it was he who appeared as the bright light and pushed me out of harm's way."

FRANCE

Nina B. wrote to tell us of the days when she was a dancer at the Lido in Paris and was rescued by an angelic being from a personal attack.

"After many hours as a performer, I would usually be very tired, and I would share a taxi home with two other dancers who lived in the same apartment building," she began her account.

"On this evening, for some reason, I felt like walking for a while through the streets of Paris. It would be dawn in a few hours, and I felt like seeing the sun come up. It seemed as though I had not seen the sunrise for many years."

As Nina walked casually, relaxing, letting herself unwind from the tensions of her performance, she became aware of the sound of footsteps behind her.

"I saw the forms of two men duck into the shadows when I stopped to turn around," she said. "Without really thinking, I had chosen to walk down streets that were not very well lighted. And although Paris is a city that never sleeps, these streets were very empty."

Not wishing to allow her fears to get the better of her, she continued to walk, putting on a small show of great confidence and assurance.

"The footsteps picked up their pace as well," she continued her story. "When I glanced quickly over my shoulder, I saw two young men following me. I could see by their gait that they had been drinking heavily. I became frightened, for I knew that alcohol would interfere with their reason and fire their passions."

Nina began to pray. "As a child I had attended convent school. For a time, my family thought that I might become a nun. If I had not so loved to dance, who knows? That night on that dark and deserted street, I began to wish that I had chosen to become a nun singing in the choir of a convent rather than a dancer in the chorus line of the Lido de Paris."

Nina said that she had always felt the presence of a guardian angel. "As a child, I was certain that I had once heard a chorus of angelic voices, and another time I was positive that I had seen an angel standing watch at my bedside."

Nina was praying for the protection of her guardian angel when the two young men caught up to her and one of them grabbed her arm.

"Their faces looked like the leering masks of demons," Nina said. "They were shouting foul things, and I could see that nothing I would say would matter to them. I began to fear for the worst."

But then suddenly a large, powerfully built man appeared directly behind Nina's assailants.

"He had huge hands, and he slammed their heads together so hard that they fell to their knees, crying out in pain as they rolled over on their backs on the sidewalk. My protector had taken away all evil thoughts from their minds with one sudden blow."

Nina thanked her rescuer profusely. "He was so plainly dressed that I assumed he must be very poor. I offered him some money, but he refused. I then suggested I buy him a meal, and he just smiled."

Nina was distracted by the sound of a taxi approaching. "I hailed the cab, and when I turned back to insist that my benefactor join me for breakfast, he was gone. I could see him nowhere on the street. It seemed impossible that anyone could have disappeared so quickly.

"But the two young men were beginning to sit up and curse, so I decided that the cab had come along just in time."

Nina got into the cab and was grateful to be able to leave the scene of what could have been a very grim episode in her life.

"I will always believe that God heard my prayer and sent a powerful angel to protect me from those two thugs," Nina concluded. "He literally appeared from nowhere and vanished in seconds. And he probably saved my life."

ITALY

Today Frank Manzetti runs a small, but successful, import-export business in Rome. According to his account, he owes his good fortune to the timely appearance of an angel.

"I was trying my best to put up a good appearance in order to gain the business support of a number of influential businessmen in Rome," he said, beginning his story. "I had practically no working capital, so I would have to obtain merchandise on credit. Once I had acquired a substantial inventory, I had great confidence that I could be successful as an exporter. As a young man, I had the opportunity to travel a great deal throughout all of Europe and overseas. I had established many good contacts that I knew would pay off if only I could convince enough companies to grant me credit."

On this fateful day in June of 1979, Frank was rushing to return to the small office space that he had rented before he received an important call from a major business contact.

"I was returning from lunch with Mr. Paccione, a small manufacturer, who said that he would extend credit to me if I could also obtain credit from Mr. Galluzzo, who had a much larger company," Manzetti said. "It was from Galluzzo that I was expecting the call. I had asked him to please call me at three o'clock. I planned to tell him that I had secured the credit and the confidence of Mr. Paccione, so would he, please, now also extend his credit to me."

Frank thought that he had allowed more than enough time to return to his office to take the call, but traffic in the city that day was even worse than usual.

"I had no secretary to answer the telephone. And, of course, in those days there were no answering machines readily available to businessmen with my kind of budget. And even if there were, it would have been in terribly poor taste to have a machine answer such an important call from such an influential person."

Frank had portrayed himself to Galluzzo as a well-established importer-exporter with an extensive inventory and experienced staff.

"I knew that I really would have these things one day soon. I had to live my dream before it had happened for the sake of my wife and three children."

But on the afternoon in June, it appeared that all was lost.

"It was ten minutes to three. There was no way that I could return to the office in less than twenty minutes. The traffic jam would cost me my dream and my future."

Frank looked at his wristwatch. He felt every second that ticked by as if it were a thorn piercing his flesh. He became nauseated. His best business suit was drenched with nervous sweat. Mr. Galluzzo was a stern-faced, no-nonsense businessman in his early sixties. He would not tolerate being asked to call at a certain time and having his call go unanswered. It would be unlikely that he would ever talk to Frank again.

"I arrived back at my office at 3:18. I had missed Galluzzo's call by eighteen minutes. I felt terrible. I didn't know what to do."

A few minutes later, after he had calmed himself to some degree, he felt that he had nothing to lose by calling the man and attempting to explain matters.

When Frank heard the sharp voice of Galluzzo's snappish secretary, he almost hung up the telephone.

"I decided to see it through. When Galluzzo came on the line, I expected his first words to come out in a roar."

Frank Manzetti got the surprise of his life.

"Ah, Frank, you managed to extricate yourself from that terrible traffic jam," Galluzzo began. "It's good to hear your voice. Do you have good news from Mr. Paccione?"

Frank was taken off guard. How did Galluzzo know about the traffic jam and his luncheon meeting with Paccione? He had wanted Galluzzo to believe that his arrangement with Paccione was one that had been well established quite some time ago.

Before Frank could respond, Galluzzo said in a whisper, "You have a fantastic secretary, Frank. What a marvelous voice and such a professional manner. Where did you ever find such a jewel? I'm really quite jealous."

Frank was dumbstruck. Finally he managed to mumble, "You spoke to my secretary?"

Galluzzo chuckled. "Who else would answer your office phone? Yes, she explained that you had called in to say that you were stuck in traffic and would be a few minutes late getting back to the office. She said that you would return my call the minute you got in. Frank, if the rest of your staff is as competent and professional as that young lady, you will have no problem in securing my full confidence and an extension of credit to put things into full operation."

Frank Manzetti was firm in his conclusion: "It could only have been an angel taking pity on me. I had no secretary, no answering service, no answering machine. Yet some very confident 'young woman' with a lovely voice and a professional manner answered my important telephone from Mr. Galluzzo and saved my future for me. There can be no other explanation."

NEW YORK

And while we're on the subject of angelic intervention over the telephone line, here is a lovely story that one of our readers sent to us about a woman we'll call Martha Jennings.

Martha Jennings was left with ten dollars to her name when her husband walked out on her, leaving her with a small baby to feed. She had lost her job weeks before. Her unemployment insurance had run out. She owed rent money. Her utilities were about to be shut off.

Martha had been advised to accept welfare, but she just could not bring herself to do it. She had worked all of her life, and she had never really been in any kind of financial I trouble until now.

But then she looked at her baby. How far would ten dollars go toward keeping the child fed?

She despised the idea of accepting a handout, yet she could see no other way.

She picked up her phone and dialed the number of the local welfare office in her area of New York City. She was surprised when the voice on the other end of the line answered with the name of a prominent business firm. She had dialed the wrong number. And the telephone company would probably disconnect her service before she could redial.

Martha could not help herself. She began to cry, and she found herself telling the stranger at the business office that she was destitute.

But Martha had found a sympathetic ear. The woman asked what experience, credentials, and qualifications she had. She immediately spoke to someone in the office, then called Martha about an hour later to say that a position requiring someone of her expertise had just opened.

"Can you come in right away for a job interview?" Martha heard the woman ask.

Martha prevailed on a neighbor to watch her baby, and she was at the firm that afternoon. She is now an executive with the company.

"I'll never believe that I dialed that number by accident," Martha Jennings said. "I know that my guardian angel guided my finger and came to my rescue during my darkest hour."

Australia

SHE WALKED WITH HER PARENTS
AND THE ANGELS IN HEAVEN

ATHERINE WAVERLEY OF CANBERRA, AUSTRALIA, told us of her journey to heaven with angelic beings while she was under the surgeon's knife in the late 1960s.

"When I entered the hospital, I knew that I was much sicker than my doctor had conceded," Katherine stated in her account of her remarkable adventure in the higher dimensions of reality.

"Two young interns saw to prepping me for surgery, and as they discussed their after-work plans, I thought about how marvelous it was to be young and to be able to plan for the future," she said. "I was forty-nine years old, and very ill, and I felt that I had come to the end of my life path."

Katherine remembers being asked to count backwards from one hundred, and then she seemed to be spinning crazily around and around.

"I heard a kind of crackling noise, like stiff paper being crunched up into a ball. Then I seemed to be bobbing like a balloon on a string. Truly, the fairest comparison that I can make is that I was a kind of shining balloon attached to my body by a silver string. I could see my body below me, and the two interns, still chattering away about their plans for the evening.

"Then I could see the surgeon, Dr. Glauser, coming down the hall, taking a last puff on a cigarette before he ground it out in an ashtray filled with white sand. He stood beside me, glanced at me, then looked me over very carefully— and became very angry. He swore at the two interns and shouted at them as if they were small, naughty boys. Nurses came running at his shouts. My body was quickly wheeled into surgery.

"*Oh, no,* I thought. *Something has gone terribly wrong. That's why I'm floating up here above everything. I must be dying.*"

Katherine remembered thinking about her husband Dennis and her two daughters, Wendy and Terry.

"I felt sad. Not for me, but for them."

As if from very far away, Katherine heard her doctor shouting at the staff, but she didn't want to watch what was going on in the operating room.

"I didn't seem to feel any more sickness or pain. I felt, somehow, as if I were finished with all that bother. It wasn't as if I no longer cared what happened to me, but I seemed to be growing more and more indifferent toward the physical me."

Then she heard bells tolling, as they do at funerals. Yes, she thought, she must indeed be quite dead.

But suddenly she heard a deep voice say, "*Not yet!*"

"And I felt myself being pulled upward and upward, like an arrow being shot into the sky!"

The next thing Katherine knew was that she was no longer a kind of shining balloon but seemed once again to be her familiar physical self. Standing before her were a number of figures in bright, glowing robes.

"The beings seemed to glow with an inner radiance," Katherine told us. "To me, they were what angels were supposed to look like, only they didn't have wings."

Katherine stood in awed silence for a moment or two before she spoke: "I am dead, then, aren't I?"

One of the angelic figures answered in a gentle, musical voice. "You may stay here for only a while, dear, then you must go back."

When Katherine remembered the heavenly experience for the account that she wrote for us, she was certain that she had seen green fields and trees and brooks and streams.

"I recall remarking how beautiful Heaven was—and then at almost precisely the same moment, I reasoned that if I were in Heaven I should be able to see my parents. In a twinkling, Mom and Dad were standing beside me, and we were all weeping tears of joy at our reunion!"

Neither of her parents appeared as old as they had when they died. Instead, Katherine told us, "both of them looked as I remembered them from my late childhood or early teenage years."

In retrospect, it seemed as though she visited with her parents for hours, even days. Then an angel in a white robe came for her and informed her that it was time for her to return.

"No sooner had the angel told me this when I was bobbing up near the ceiling of a hospital room. I was shocked to hear Father Galvin giving me the last rites! My husband and daughters were crying, and my sister Donna was there. A nurse stood at the left side of the bed with her fingers on my pulse."

Once again Katherine heard that same deep voice: "*It is not yet your time!*"

"And I heard that same weird, crackling noise. I saw the color of blood all around me—and I was back in my body!"

Katherine moaned with the pain of the illness and the recently completed surgery. When she opened her eyes, Dennis, Wendy, Terry, Donna, and Father Galvin were smiling at her.

"All the saints be praised," Father Galvin said. "Our Katy is back among us."

The priest asked the nurse to summon Dr. Glauser to examine her.

As soon as she regained command of her tongue, Katherine told everyone that she had gone to Heaven with the angels and that she had seen her deceased parents.

Later, Katherine learned why no one seemed surprised by her statement. "After the surgery, Dr. Glauser had given me only a few hours to pass the crisis point or to die. Father Galvin had been called by Dennis to administer the last rites, because my chances to live seemed almost nonexistent.

"I know that my experience with the angels in Heaven was genuine," Katherine concluded. "I know that my family believes me, as well."

Austria

UR LATE FRIEND J. WOLFGANG WEILGART first met an angelic being when he was a child of six in his native Austria.

Many years later, with doctoral degrees in linguistics and psychology from the universities of Vienna and Heidelberg, he described for us the mystical moment in his childhood when a stranger in a "star-strewn mantle" appeared to him. It was this angelic visitation, Dr. Weilgart stated, that inspired him to devote his life to a new unity of humankind. In that moment of awe and reverence he felt a "cosmic lifestream" enter him, as if his former life had been dissolved.

When Wolfgang told his parents of his experience, they sent him to a psychiatrist, who found the six-year-old's only abnormality to be the fact that he could solve academic problems at the level of a thirteen-year-old. His Binet IQ tested above 200. The psychiatrist warned Wolfgang that in Western society uncommon experiences may be told only as dreams or in poems.

Later, as a young scholar, Weilgart wrote his first doctoral dissertation on "Creation and Contemplation." His paper was one of the few outspoken pacifist arguments against Hitler and the whole Nazi ideology of aggressive action.

Weilgart's father, Dr. Hofrat Weilgartner, had worked for the *Anschluss* (the annexation of Austria by Germany), and so the Nazis expected similar cooperation from the son. The Nazis offered Weilgart a high position in their secret service because of his fluency in a dozen different languages, his knowledge of psychology, and his friendship with the underground—against whom they wished him to be an informer. But he had received another of his cosmic communications from the angel in the "star-strewn mantle." He spent an afternoon and an evening wrapped in solitary contemplation, seeking guidance from his heavenly advisor. Although a position in the intelligence corps would have been the only way to rehabilitate himself in the eyes of the Nazis, whom he had offended by his doctoral dissertation, Weilgart refused.

His angelic guide warned him that the Gestapo were keeping him under close watch. "Flee to Holland at once," the cosmic voice told him.

Weilgart had few friends whom he could trust, and no connections with practical helpers. His parents had filled his pockets with money, but so much cash was a sign of one who was seeking to flee the country.

Following his inner, angelic voice, he encountered a stranger near the border whom he felt he could trust. He gave the man all of his funds, together with his parents' address, and asked him to send the money to the Weilgartner residence. Although the stranger could have suspected Weilgart of flight, turned him in to the Gestapo, and kept the money for himself, the man (perhaps an angel in disguise) did as he had been requested.

As Weilgart approached the border, he encountered a Gestapo patrol, who were searching everyone who wished to leave or enter the country. The guard blocked his path and demanded to see his identity papers. Weilgart knew that an order to arrest him had been issued by the Gestapo.

And then, once again, just as had occurred when he was a boy of six, he felt a "cosmic lifestream" entering his body. To his great surprise, Weilgart suddenly heard *his own voice* ordering the Gestapo patrol to leave their station at the border and assume another assignment.

To his astonishment, the patrol obeyed his sharp commands, as if he wore the uniform of a high-ranking officer rather than a rumpled business suit. Without another word, the very Gestapo border patrol that had been assigned to arrest him walked quietly away and allowed him to cross the border without the slightest interference.

Although the scholar made good his flight to Holland, it was not long before that nation was being invaded by the Nazis, who would execute Weilgart as a deserter if they should discover his exact whereabouts.

The young mystic's inner voice brought him to the Dutch governor of Java, who happened to be visiting in The Hague. The governor listened to Weilgart's predicament, then sat down, wrote a visa for him, and presented him with a ship ticket to America. In the meantime, somebody had sent Weilgart's poems to German expatriate Thomas Mann, who, as a Nobel Prize-winner and an honorary doctor at the University of California, was able to arrange for him to receive a postdoctoral research fellowship to write his book *Shakespeare Psychognostic.*

Dr. John Wolfgang Weilgart had at last escaped the Nazi threat to freedom and arrived in the United States, where the mission of peace, love, and brotherhood assigned to him by his angelic guide could receive a much fuller expression.

Canada

SHE RECEIVED AN ANGELIC DONATION
TO FEED HER HUNGRY GIRLS

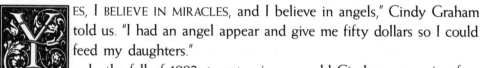ES, I BELIEVE IN MIRACLES, and I believe in angels," Cindy Graham told us. "I had an angel appear and give me fifty dollars so I could feed my daughters."

In the fall of 1992, twenty-nine-year-old Cindy was moving from Edmonton, Alberta, to Toronto, Ontario, with the promise that a cousin could help her find suitable employment. Her husband Dwight had been killed in an automobile accident, and his meager insurance policies had barely provided enough money for a burial.

"I was down to my last few dollars," Cindy told us. "I just couldn't find the kind of job that would allow me to support my children and still have enough money to get a decent apartment in a good neighborhood. When my second cousin Charlene said that she could find a good job for me, I decided to gamble the last bit of money I had left on a bus trip to Toronto."

Cindy had packed some peanut butter sandwiches and a small bag of potato chips for the bus trip, but they didn't last the three of them very long.

"Margie was only six and Mindy was just four. I couldn't stand it when they would cry because they were hungry. I also knew that they would probably develop motion sickness a lot faster if their little stomachs were empty. It seemed like we had barely started the long bus ride when our food was gone. I promised them I would get them something good to eat at Winnipeg, but I knew that I was down to my last three dollars. I didn't know how we would last all the way to Toronto."

Cindy finally got the girls to sleep after they divided the last half of a peanut butter sandwich.

"There were only a few passengers on board at that point in the trip, but I figured the bus would fill up after the Winnipeg stop. I have never had to beg for anything in my life, but I thought an elderly man sitting toward the back looked kind. I sat quietly for several minutes, trying to get up the courage to ask him for just a few dollars for the girls."

Before she got to her feet to make the humiliating journey to the back of the bus with her mental begging bowl in hand, Cindy began to pray.

"I asked God to have mercy on us. I asked if I could somehow get just enough money to buy the girls a decent meal. I knew Charlene would lend me some money when we got to Toronto, but I had been too ashamed to ask her for any money for the trip. I told God that I just had to have some money. Margie and Mindy would be starved and sick long before we reached our final destination."

By the time she had finished praying, Cindy was crying.

"That's when I felt someone touch me on the shoulder. I turned around to see a beautiful lady all dressed in white. At first her whole body seemed to be outlined with a thin, bright light. Then the light kept growing until she was completely enveloped in this magnificent illumination. Suddenly it seemed as if I were somewhere on a cloud way up in the sky instead of on a bus."

Cindy remembered that the beautiful lady told her not to worry. "'Your life is going to be so much better now,' she told me. 'You and the girls are going to be just fine. Know that God is good, and we, the angels, keep watch over you always. Know also, that we love you.'"

With those words, the angel disappeared.

"But I had tangible proof that she had been there," Cindy said. "A crisp new fifty-dollar bill was sticking out of my blouse pocket!"

Cindy saw that the bus driver seemed to be watching her in the rearview mirror. She wondered if he had seen the angel manifest.

"Is everything all right, ma'am?" he asked.

"Did you see the beautiful lady in white who was standing behind me?" Cindy wanted to know.

The driver shook his head. "No, I surely didn't. There was no lady standing behind you, beautiful or otherwise. But you seemed to be acting strangely, like you were troubled or sick or something."

Cindy smiled broadly. "I was troubled, thank you, sir. But I'm not anymore. I know that God and the angels are looking out for me."

"Glad to hear it," he said, giving her a crooked smile. "Hope they look in on me once in a while, too."

"You can bank on it," Cindy told him, clutching the fifty dollars of Heaven-sent help. When the bus pulled into Winnipeg, she would be able to buy the girls a nice, warm meal The long trip to Toronto would seem a lot shorter with food in their stomachs. They had been provided for by an angel.

China

ICHAEL CHANG HAD CONVERTED to Christianity and had been baptized by a Lutheran missionary in 1936. He had chosen his Christian name after the Archangel Michael, and he had become such an enthusiastic convert that he had opened a store in Tsingkiangpu, Kiangsu Province, that featured Bibles, religious books, hymnals, and other inspirational items.

In 1942 the Imperial Japanese Army had won their war against China; among their objectives was the removal and confiscation of all Christian materials. Chang knew that it was only a matter of time before his shop would be stripped of its inventory. Most of the shop owners of his acquaintance had already been visited by Japanese marines who loaded all Christian-oriented items onto a truck. One of the shopkeepers, who had protested the act, had been severely beaten.

And then came the day that Chang had dreaded. It was early afternoon when a Japanese truck with five marines stopped in front of his shop. The truck was already half-filled with Christian books, Bibles, and religious tracts. The marines jumped off the truck and began to walk toward the front door.

But just as they approached the entrance, a well-dressed Chinese man stepped directly in their path and entered the shop ahead of them. Strangely enough, the five marines stopped just outside the door.

Nervously, Chang anticipated the onslaught of the Japanese marines, but he noticed that they had mysteriously halted their invasion of his shop. Incredibly, they seemed to be waiting for the Chinese gentleman to leave.

Chang directed his attention to the man who had entered his establishment. With the war over and China defeated, he could not imagine any Chinese, rich or poor, who would be respected by any member of the Japanese forces of occupation.

"M-may I help you, sir?" Chang did not recognize the man, though he did know by name nearly every customer who had ever patronized his shop. This man was a total stranger.

The man smiled at him kindly. "I would like to look at the Christian tracts that you have. Have you any on prayer?"

Chang nodded, leading the customer toward a bookshelf in the corner. "Yes, there are a number of tracts on the subject. And I have some excellent books on prayer, as well."

The man took his time browsing through the various books and tracts.

Chang kept one eye on the soldiers at the door, the other on his customer. The man was dressed in a very expensive suit of finest quality. Money would certainly not appear to be a factor in his taking his time to study the printed materials.

When Chang managed a furtive glance at his watch, he was astonished to see that the stranger had been in his shop for nearly two hours.

And still the Japanese marines had not entered to confiscate the Christian materials. They loitered outside the door; they pressed their noses against the windows to look inside; but they did not enter.

"What do those men want?" the stranger asked.

Chang told him that the Japanese were confiscating all Christian reading material. They had come to take away all of his stock of Bibles, hymnals, tracts, and other books.

"Then I think it would be wise of us to kneel and pray that they go away," the man said, as if it were a simple task to banish five Japanese marines as it would be to brush away five bothersome insects.

The stranger took Chang's hand in his and they knelt to pray.

When the Japanese marines climbed back into the truck and drove away, the two men had been praying for ninety minutes.

Soon after they heard the sound of the truck driving away, the well-dressed Chinese gentleman got to his feet and indicated that Chang should do likewise.

"What you must do now, Michael," the stranger said, "is to load up as many books and tracts as you can and hide them away before the Japanese return. People will need the comfort and inspiration of these materials during the difficult days ahead."

With those words, the man left Chang's shop.

Before Chang could puzzle through any of the extraordinary events of the afternoon, Benny Lee, a Christian friend, ran into his shop. "Michael, are you all right? Where are all the soldiers? Was there a fight? Was anyone hurt?"

Chang placed a tranquil hand on Benny's shoulder. "Calm down. I'm fine. The Japanese soldiers left. It was a miracle."

Benny laughed, then quickly sobered. "A miracle of might, my friend. But you must get out of here and take your soldier friends with you before those Japanese marines return with reinforcements."

Chang shook his head in confusion. "What 'soldier friends' are you talking about, Benny?"

"Why, the twelve who protected you all afternoon, of course!"

When Chang finally convinced his friend that he did not know what he was talking about, Benny explained that he had been standing quietly outside near the Japanese truck. He had heard the Japanese marines complaining that they were outnumbered and inadequately armed to enter the store and face the twelve tough-looking Chinese soldiers who stood shoulder-to-shoulder inside. Bands of Chinese guerrilla fighters still resisted the invasion of their homeland, and the Japanese marines were reluctant to face their wrath for the sake of a few Bibles.

"They decided to attempt to wait out the Chinese soldiers, thinking they would soon vacate your shop and leave them to their task of confiscating your inventory," Benny said. "But after nearly four hours of waiting outside, they finally gave up. But you know they'll return soon with more men."

Chang told his friend that there had been no Chinese guerrilla fighters in his store. "The stranger who prayed with me must have been an angel with heavenly powers from God who made those marines think that they saw my shop full of angry soldiers."

Chang remembered the angelic visitor's parting admonition to secret away as many inspirational materials as possible for the days of trial ahead. He agreed with Benny that the Japanese would soon come back with reinforcements, and he asked him to help him carry off as many books and tracts as possible before they returned.

Michael Chang often told the story of his angelic visitor during the years of Japanese occupation, and his remarkable account gave many men and women the inspiration they needed to survive the time of tribulation.

Denmark

THE ANGEL BOARDED THE TRAIN WITH SAD NEWS

OLFE LUDVIGSEN, ONE OF OUR CORRESPONDENTS from Denmark, provided us with an account of an angel that appeared to his mother and him on board a train when he was a small boy.

"It was in the winter of 1953," Rolfe said. "My maternal grandmother had developed cancer, and I was accompanying my mother on a journey to visit her. Grandmother Larsen lived in a small village near the German border, and since we lived up north in Frederikshavn, it was quite a long train ride in those days."

Although he was only a child, Rolfe knew that his mother was very concerned about Grandmother Larsen. "I had heard her discussing the situation with my father before we left home. She was afraid that the cancer had spread, and she wanted to bring Grandmother back with us to receive better medical attention in a larger city."

To make matters even worse on the trip, Rolfe could tell that his mother was very uncomfortable on the train. "I knew that she had to be exhausted, but she seemed unable to relax or to fall asleep."

The two of them had been sitting quietly when they saw a woman dressed in white enter the door at the end of their coach.

"I remember well her features," Rolfe said. "She was extremely beautiful, with unusually large blue eyes. Dressed completely in white, she seemed almost to be shining. She seemed quite tall, and I knew that she was looking directly at my mother and me."

Rolfe recalled feeling uneasy and asking his mother about the lady who had just entered their coach: "Do you know her, Mother? She seems to be staring at us."

Before his mother could answer, the woman walked up the aisle and took the seat opposite them. She smiled warmly, and then spoke directly to his mother, addressing her by her first name. "I have a message for you, Klara," she said.

Rolfe remembered his mother frowning in puzzlement and shifting in her seat. "Do I know you?" she asked the stranger. "Have we ever met?"

The woman nodded to Rolfe's mother, and then said, "I have always known you, Klara." Then the beautiful stranger placed her palms over his mother's trembling hands and said, "I will soon come for your mother, dear. I will take her home with me."

Rolfe recalled how his mother began to weep and shake her head in protest. "Who...who are you? Why do you say such things to me?"

The tall woman smiled down at them as she rose to leave. "You know who I am. I'll not see you again until the day when I come to take you home, dear Klara."

With those words, Rolfe said, the lovely, statuesque woman turned, walked to the end of the coach, and stepped out of the door.

Rolfe tried his best to comfort his weeping mother by putting his, little arms around her neck and hugging her.

"What has so upset your mother, boy?" asked the woman in the seat behind them. "Is she ill?"

"The lady in white said some things that made her cry," Rolfe replied.

"What lady in white?" the woman wanted to know. "There's no such woman in this coach."

Rolfe tried his best to explain. "She's not seated in this coach, but she came in and sat opposite us for a while. She just left…only minutes ago. You must have seen her."

The woman scowled and shook her head. "I'm directly behind you, boy. I saw no woman dressed in white sitting with you for even a second. There's been no such lady in this coach."

By now, other passengers had joined in the conversation. Everyone firmly denied having seen a beautiful woman in white enter the coach and sit opposite Mrs. Ludvigsen and her son. Rolfe said that he will never forget his childish anger and frustration with the men and women as, one by one, they all refuted his account of the strange lady.

On the brink of tears, he asked his mother for confirmation and support. After all, it was *she* who had been brought to tears by their mysterious visitor. "She was here, wasn't she, Mommy?"

"She answered me in a soft whisper that I will hear in my mind all the rest of my life," Rolfe said. "'She was the Angel of Death, my dear son. She was kind enough to prepare me for the death of Grandmother Larsen. Pray that you do not see that particular angel again for many, many years.'"

According to Rolfe, his grandmother passed away three days after they had arrived. "I know that Mother was much better able to bear the emotional pain because of the forewarning that she had received from the beautiful angel on the train. Mother is nearly eighty. Although she knows a return visit from the lovely woman in white is inevitable, she has told me that she is in no hurry to meet her again."

Egypt

APOLEON BONAPARTE ENTERED the history books long ago as a renowned military strategist and the emperor of France. The legend of his experience with angels, however, is often forgotten. It is said that according to his own testimony Napoleon was visited by a messenger from Heaven who predicted his downfall if he did not curb his lust for power.

At the beginning of his rise to prominence, the soldier-statesman was characterized by his goals of virtue, truth, and justice. But when he realized the elusiveness of these ideals, Napoleon appeared to become obsessed with a shameless desire to conquer the world. Illustrating that angels recognize no human land boundaries, Napoleon received his first angelic warning in Egypt from an angel who identified himself as a guardian of the French nation. The account of the angel's international journey follows.

IN 1798, THE VERY PYRAMIDS of Egypt trembled as Napoleon's troops defeated the ten thousand horsemen of the Muslim chief Mourad Bey. Blood saturated the sand as the French routed the Muslims. It seemed at this point as if all of

Egypt—and even all of Africa—lay within the grasp of the diminutive military genius.

Napoleon took over Mourad Bey's palace and claimed the extravagant master bedroom as his own. He commanded that he be left alone to enjoy the splendor in solitude, free at last from the responsibilities of his position and the incessant demands of his officers. That night, he slept soundly until near dawn, when a movement in the room awakened him.

Heavy with sleep, his eyes gradually focused on a tall figure dressed entirely in red. "You, sir, are an intruder," Napoleon said angrily. "I demand that you leave at once."

"Draw not your weapon. It will be useless against me," the intruder said in a sepulchral voice. "I am the Red Man. I am the angel who has appeared before the rulers of France for many centuries."

Napoleon was transfixed as the strange visitor continued.

"You are obsessed with power," the being scowled, "and you think not of your people."

Napoleon protested strenuously. "Everything I do is for the good of my subjects."

The Red Man's hollow laughter echoed in the elegant bedroom. "You are an ambitious man. You wish to play God with the destiny of France and all of humanity.

"I know you better than you know yourself," the mysterious stranger went on. "I walked beside you during your quiet, solitary walks when you were a schoolboy at Brienne. Even then you had the magnificent vision of founding an empire that would eclipse all those previously known. I have walked silently beside you as you marched against the armies of Austria on the plains of Italy. And today when the horsemen of Mourad Bey were crushed beneath your heel, you envisioned yourself as master of an Oriental throne."

"And why not?" Napoleon demanded. "I have conquered Egypt, and even now my ships lie in the harbor of Alexandria."

The angel shook his head. "Your ships are *not* in the harbor of Alexandria. Your order was not obeyed. If your own officers rebel against you, how can you hope to conquer the world?"

"You lie!" Napoleon shouted. "How could you know such things?"

The Red Man's eyes narrowed in impatience. "In less than a year you will return to France having failed to conquer Egypt. The might of England, Russia, and Turkey will be allied against you. France will soon be in a state of chaos."

"Nonsense!" Napoleon sneered. "Should France ever be in trouble, I will return and overthrow the miserable officials responsible for such a disgrace."

The angel turned and began to leave. "I have warned you," he said before he made his exit. "Curb your ambition and heed the threats of your opponents. Control your lust for absolute power before you perish without friends or a country. I leave you now."

As every student of history knows, Napoleon's Egyptian campaign failed. The prophecy of the Red Man, the angelic messenger whose manifestation had been recorded by many French monarchs before Napoleon, was fulfilled precisely as he had warned the feisty Corsican.

ELEVEN YEARS LATER, on a foggy morning in 1809, Napoleon's muddy black boots stomped across the luxurious carpet in an Austrian palace. The French army had decimated the Austrian troops at the brutal battle of Wagram, and now Napoleon prepared to dictate his harsh terms of peace for the defeated nation.

At midnight, as he dozed at a desk covered by maps dotted with colored pins, he was awakened by the Red Man.

In the same deep, hollow voice, the being again identified himself as a messenger from Heaven. "I come to warn you that unless you cease your present campaigns at once, you will be utterly destroyed. You have just four years to accomplish complete peace in Europe. Four years, no more." The angel vanished.

Napoleon told a number of his aides about the mysterious Red Man, then chose to dismiss the incident and continue with the stern realities of his war machine.

THE RED MAN MADE HIS THIRD and final appearance to the Emperor Napoleon on January 1, 1814. Napoleon was afflicted with legions of enemies, both in France and in the nations allied against him. Although he had shut himself up with orders that absolutely no one was to disturb him, the angel manifested before him once again. The Red Man told him that it would be all over for him in three months unless he made immediate peace.

"That's impossible," Napoleon complained. "I need more time."

The angel admonished him sternly. "You must negotiate a peace in three months or you will be disgraced."

"A year," Napoleon tried to bargain. "I cannot do as you ask. It is impossible."

"I cannot be swayed by human entreaties," the angel said firmly. "I am but a messenger whose sole mission is to warn you as I am instructed."

"Grant me a year," the Emperor pleaded.

"Three months," the Red Man repeated before vanishing.

THE FOLLOWING WEEKS WERE DISASTROUS for Napoleon. In an imprudent move, he left Paris unprotected while he took his armies on a campaign to the east. The allied forces moved into the city and captured it. Mobs formed in the streets. The empire crumbled.

Exactly three months after his final conversation with the Red Man, the National Assembly held a secret meeting and demanded Napoleon's abdication.

England

His Guardian Angel Twice Saved His Life

RTHUR MONTGOMERY OF TUNBRIDGE WELLS, KENT, saw his guardian angel for the first time when he was a boy of ten during the Battle of Britain in 1940.

"Our family spent nights in a nearby public air raid shelter," Arthur said. "Grandfather Pearson insisted that if he were going to die under Nazi bombs, he wanted to perish in his own house, not trapped with hundreds in a hole in the ground; but Mother always managed to drag him along with us."

Arthur's father was away in the army, but his uncle Lawrence joined the Air Raid Precautions for night duty, and the boy sometimes managed to talk his way into going along.

"On this particular night, the Nazi bombers seemed to appear out of nowhere," Arthur remembered. "Suddenly the sirens were howling, and within minutes bombs began to fall close at hand. In the confusion, I became separated from Uncle Lawrence."

Uncertain whether to try to make a dash for the public shelter where he knew his mother and grandfather were huddled with hundreds of others, Arthur weighed his options. He could see a sturdy-looking house that he knew was quite deserted but could provide a safe haven. Or there was an old brick toolshed just down the block that would offer room enough for a ten-year-old to be secure.

"I knew that I must decide quickly. Bombs were screaming down within a few hundred yards of me and getting even closer."

Arthur decided on the deserted house and made a run for it.

"But just as I entered the door, I was met by a most imposing figure of a tall, silver-haired man dressed in a white robe. 'Leave this place at once,' he ordered me in a deep, commanding voice. 'It will be bombed in seconds. Run quickly to the toolshed. You will be safe there!' And then, that quickly, he disappeared."

Arthur was barely inside the toolshed when bombs blasted the house into rubble and sent shrapnel and bricks clattering down on roofs and streets.

"Mother was furious with Uncle Lawrence when we were all united later that evening," Arthur said. "I made it quite clear that I was the one to blame, not poor Uncle. And besides, the important thing was that we were all alive—and that I had most certainly met, and been saved by, my guardian angel."

ARTHUR WAS NOT PRIVILEGED to encounter his guardian angel again until forty years had gone by.

"It was 1980, and I was now fifty years old and running to catch a bus," Arthur said. "It seemed as though I was about to make the stop before it pulled away when I distinctly felt something tugging at my coat and slowing me down. In my peripheral vision I was astonished to see the form of a tall man holding on to my coat."

Fearing that a mugger was attempting to rob him, Arthur spun around, holding his briefcase at chest level.

"I was about to slam the case into my attacker's face when I was startled to behold my silver-haired, white-robed guardian angel. 'It's you!' was all I could manage to say."

Never one to waste or to mince words, the angelic being came right to the point. "If you had kept running after that bus, you would have had a heart attack. Go straight away to your physician. Now!"

Once again, his cosmic benefactor disappeared as quickly as he had materialized. But Arthur was as obedient as he had been when he was a ten-year-old boy surviving the Battle of Britain.

"I figured if the blessed fellow was right then, he was right now," Arthur said. "Although I felt well enough, my physician said that my image of excellent health was an illusion maintained because I had not slowed down enough to listen to my body. According to him, if I had not come in to have my heart and cholesterol and so forth checked when I did, and had not begun a proper medical regimen, Mother Nature would have slowed me down with a heart attack. Once again, my guardian angel had saved my life."

AN ANGEL SENDS AN EXPECTANT MOTHER TO A BETTER DOCTOR

In the mid-1930s, Rev. Maurice Elliott of Lincolnshire published a small book entitled *A Modern Miracle*, in which he related the extraordinary details of the appearance of an angel messenger who manifested to save the lives of his wife and their unborn child. Mrs. Elliott's attending medical physician had assured her that her life and that of her baby would be certain to be snuffed out if she did not submit to the operation that he prescribed.

A specialist, summoned to offer a second opinion, agreed with the Elliotts' doctor that the only chance the expectant mother had of recovery was to undergo the surgery at once—even if "the result would be doubtful."

Reverend Elliott and his wife were extremely nervous about the recommended surgery, and felt a profound lack of confidence in their regular physician's ability to perform the operation safely and successfully. They began to pray earnestly for God's guidance.

That night in their home, a spiritual messenger, a "tall man of fine physique, attired in dazzling white garments," suddenly appeared before Reverend and Mrs. Elliott. The angel told them to travel to the office of a surgeon named Thomas Pearson, who practiced in Brighton, forty miles away. This doctor, the angel promised them, had the necessary skill to perform the required operation without risk to either mother or child.

The couple obediently followed the heavenly being's instructions, with the result that both the mother and her baby were saved.

Reverend Elliott's book included affidavits signed by his wife, by Dr. Pearson, and by an eminent gynecologist—all vouching for the truth of the appearance of the angelic messenger and the success of the subsequent surgery.

In 1936, in his massive work of research entitled *Does Man Survive?*, George Lindsay Johnson included his interview with Reverend Elliott regarding additional details of the above story.

"The angel messenger was a man of very fine physique and above the average height," Reverend Elliott told Johnson. "His age appeared to be about forty years. His eyes, hair, and voice were full of life; in fact, he radiated life. In comparison with him, we are 'existing' rather than 'living.' I cannot describe his presence; it was electric.

"He appeared to us after we had asked God to send us help. He came in answer to our prayers, and he promised to lead us to a surgeon who would take care of 'the little sleeper within.' He told us to go to Brighton and to seek out a surgeon named Dr. Thomas Pearson."

Once the Elliotts had traveled to Brighton, the angel met them there and guided them to a hotel at which the surgeon happened to be staying.

"After Dr. Pearson had finished talking to us," Reverend Elliott told Johnson, "the angel walked with us back to the train station. He wore sandals and seemed to pass through matter, i.e., through the people who passed by close to us on the journey. He was invisible to all but us.

"He finally gave us parting instructions and vanished suddenly, but not without saying good-bye."

Mrs. Elliot confidently returned to Brighton for her surgery on the appointed date, secure in the knowledge that the surgical skills of Dr. Pearson had received the highest of recommendations.

France

Her Trip to Heaven Inspired Her to Return to Painting

N August 1990, while on holiday in Toulon in southeastern France, thirty-two-year-old Tina Moncrief of Reims took a nasty fall down a steep cliff and suffered a severely fractured skull, a broken leg, and several cracked ribs. The two German hikers who discovered her limp body thought at first that she was dead.

"Once I was brought to the hospital, I slipped in and out of consciousness for two or three days," Tina wrote in her account of her experience. "During those first two days when, indeed, I was just barely clinging to life, I was given a magnificent glimpse of paradise by my guardian angel.

"Immediately after the fall, I felt my spirit leaving my body. I seemed at first to be spinning, then rising higher and higher until I could view my crumpled body on the rocks below."

Tina assumed that she had been killed and that her soul was leaving her body. "I saw what appeared to be a very long, dark tunnel. I seemed to be drawn toward it, and I felt a brief moment of fear as I supposed that I was entering the final darkness of death and the loss of all consciousness."

But then Tina saw a door in the tunnel with bright light coming from it. As she drew nearer, she could hear the distinct sounds of choral music floating toward her.

"I felt very comforted and no longer afraid. And then I saw my guardian angel. Although the angelic being was tall, commanding, and glowing with a soft illumination, I somehow recognized it by its energy as the elderly woman who had suddenly appeared to pull me out of the path of a speeding automobile when I was seven."

Tina said that she could not determine the gender of her angel guardian. "Even its voice was somehow devoid of any distinctive male or female intonation, but the words that the being spoke to me were very calming, very inspirational. I felt so much love emanating from this wonderful, compassionate angel."

As Tina glanced at the heavenly environment around them, she saw lovely green meadows, stately trees, numerous angelic beings, and a wide variety of animals. "My section of paradise looked very much like a super-enriched Earth. The colors seemed brighter and richer. Everything seemed to be stepped-up in intensity."

After she felt she had been living in Heaven for at least a week, her guardian angel surprised her by saying that she was only visiting paradise for a short while.

"It is not yet your time, my child," the lovely entity said. "We've only brought you here for a few Earth hours so that you can be 'out of the way,' so to speak, while the doctors work on your body and your physical self begins to restore itself."

Tina felt a rush of disappointment. She liked it there. And her life in Reims as a secretary really hadn't been going anywhere special.

"You've needed this time to slow your pace," the angel told her. "You came into this world with a great talent for painting. You gave up your art to follow business pursuits which really haven't worked out all that well for you."

Tina acknowledged the truth of the angel's assessment of her life to the present time.

"Now, my dear," her guardian angel smiled, "while you are recuperating from your injuries, you will have plenty of time to resume painting."

Once again everything went black.

"When I opened my eyes, a nurse was calling my name," Tina remembered. "My consciousness returned to pain, but in spite of my injuries and my discomfort, I was filled with a renewed enthusiasm for life."

As soon as she was able to sit up, Tina gave a nurse money to buy her some colored pencils and a sketch pad. By the time she was released from the hospital, she was ready to begin transforming blank canvas into brilliant portraits of heavenly beings with her paintbrushes.

"At present," she concluded, "I am forced by my financial condition to be an after-work and weekend painter. However, I know within my heart that I will soon be able to paint portraits of angels and heavenly scenes as my lifework."

NOSTRADAMUS AND THE PROPHECIES OF THE ANGEL ANAEL

Although the prophet Nostradamus has become very well known, few people are aware that the mystic received his world-famous prophecies from an angel. Interestingly, even the most detailed and distinguished of the documentaries depicting Nostradamus's life neglect to mention the source of his futuristic inspirations.

ON DECEMBER 14, 1503, in Saint-Remy in Provence, Michel de Nostredame began a life that was destined to be filled with political intrigue, Renaissance rationalism, and prophetic writings. Sometime before his birth, his Jewish parents decided to become Catholics because of a papal edict decreeing disfavor to all who were not Christians. By the time Michel was a young man, the religious practice of the family had become a curious mixture of Catholic and Jewish customs and belief constructs, blended with a generous dose of mysticism.

When he was old enough, Nostradamus was sent off to study liberal arts at Avignon. Although he was most interested in studying the stars, his practical-minded father insisted that he become a man of medicine.

After four years of intensive study in Parisian medical schools, Nostradamus passed his examination and was allowed to establish a practice. His practice was disrupted when the Black Death struck Southern France.

The young doctor was considered very successful in his treatment of the plague, and he gained a reputation as a great healer. Later, he returned to academia, earned his doctorate, and accepted a position at the university. His unquenchable desire to travel and to seek out esoteric wisdom made him unhappy in a university setting, but by now he had a wife and two children, and his deep affection for his family enabled him to achieve some level of contentment.

When another outbreak of the plague took his wife and children, Nostradamus was grief-stricken. He who had saved so many lives from the Black Death had been unable to keep his own family safe from its deadly embrace. He abandoned his medical practice and set about wandering across Europe.

It was during this period that he discovered that the angel Anael was guiding him and blessing him with prophetic powers.

As he wandered from city to city, Nostradamus began to make predictions that made him famous. While in Italy, he saw a young Franciscan monk approaching his party. Although his companions commented that the young cleric was but an ex-swineherd named Felice Peretti, the prophet bent one knee to the ground as he passed. Afterward, when questioned about his strange behavior, Nostradamus answered solemnly that he must submit himself and bend a knee before His Holiness. The puzzling reply was not made clear to Nostradamus's friends until 1585, when Cardinal Peretti became Pope Sixtus V.

NOSTRADAMUS BEGAN TO WRITE almost exclusively in poetic quatrains not long after he was brought to the court of France by Catherine de' Medici, the Queen Mother. She was concerned for her children and she demanded that the prophet disclose their future.

We can imagine the angel Anael whispering in his ear that he must proceed with caution on such dangerous ground. In a prophetic flash from the angel, Nostradamus was shown that all the children were destined to die young as the result of political intrigues.

Nostradamus quietly absorbed the inner vision that Anael disclosed. He stood before the Queen Mother, searching for some appropriate manner in which to express such tragedy. It would be sheer folly to predict to the ruthless Catherine de' Medici that her progeny were destined for miserable deaths.

And then, with Anael's guidance, the words came—all of them accurate, but couched in obscure poetic language.

The Queen Mother seemed satisfied to be left to interpret the mystical verses, and Nostradamus left the palace with his head still attached to his neck. He had received Anael's inspiration to begin to cloak ugly truths in poetic utterance— and thus preserve his own skin.

Honduras

AN ANGEL SENT HIS SOUL BACK TO HIS BODY

HONDURAN GILBERT LOPEZ TOLD US of the time that he became very ill when he had been living in the coastal city of La Ceiba.

"Although my body seemed incapable of movement, my senses essentially remained alert and aware," he said. "My wife Guadalupe and my best friend, Dr. Claudio Cardoza, kept a faithful vigil at my bedside. From time to time other friends would stop by to visit only briefly, and I watched their grim faces as they beheld my desperate condition."

At the point when Dr. Cardoza was nearly exhausted from maintaining a regular physician's schedule as well as spending long hours at Gilbert's bedside, a cheery Catholic nurse from the United States volunteered to help keep watch.

"Sister Veronica's arrival could not have been better timed," Gilbert said. "I was beginning to worry more about my friend Claudio's collapsing from fatigue than I was about my own condition."

Gilbert remembered that he had been quite aware that he might die. "But I was not afraid. I was simply astonished that I was lying there so helplessly on my bed. The illness had come on so quickly that I had not had time mentally to prepare myself for the possibilities of death or a long period of convalescence."

One night, as his condition was worsening, Gilbert heard Sister Veronica telling Guadalupe that he must have a transfusion of plasma. "She went on to say that she knew of only one bottle of that precious fluid available in the entire town."

Several hours later, Dr. Cardoza and Sister Veronica were able to give Gilbert the needed transfusion—but then he went into shock. "I have dim memories of shivering violently. It seemed as though the slightest movement brought undue stress on my heart. *And then my heart stopped completely!*"

At that moment, Gilbert became aware that there seemed to be two versions of himself present in the room. There was the pale, sweat-drenched, slack-jawed creature lying on the bed. And there was the Real Gilbert standing off to the side, somehow aware of everyone's thoughts and feelings.

"My wife was crying. Claudio sighed deeply and tears came to his eyes. 'We've lost him,' he said softly."

Sister Veronica was still bending over Gilbert's body. "No, he will come back. I do not think that it is his time to die. I do not think God will take him at this time."

Sister Veronica's faith appeared to be stronger than her medical knowledge. "I wanted to tell her that it was all right. I was at peace. But then I became aware of a beautiful angel in a long, flowing robe standing at my right side. I could not tell the sex of the entity, and even its voice seemed genderless. Waves of rainbow-hued light emanated from a brilliantly illuminated arc around its head. I assumed that I had died and was being met by my guardian angel, but the entity smiled at me and said, 'Your time is not yet completed. You have much more work to do. You must return to your body.'"

A part of Gilbert's consciousness watched Dr. Cardoza injecting something into his arm. "I learned later that the injection was his last, desperate attempt to start my heart beating again. Frantically, Sister Veronica began searching for a pulse. 'I've got one!' she shouted in triumph."

Gilbert said that it was as if he were returning to his body from the very farthest reaches of the universe. "It took me quite a while to return to full consciousness, but I knew that I would not die. My guardian angel stayed with me until I spoke my first words, asking if I might have a sip of water."

Guadalupe clutched his hand, her face wet with tears. "We were so afraid that we had lost you!"

Claudio grasped his other hand. "You came back to us, my dear friend!"

In a hoarse whisper, Gilbert agreed. "My guardian angel heeded Sister Veronica's diagnosis. It was not yet time for me to return home to Heaven."

Hungary

ANGELS SENT A VISION OF AN ASSASSINATION
THAT CHANGED THE COURSE OF WORLD HISTORY

ANY SCHOLARS OF RELIGIOUS EXPERIENCE believe that one of the most amazing prophetic dreams in our century was sent by the angels on June 28, 1914, to Dr. Josef von Lanyi, a Roman Catholic bishop in Hungary. The dream proved to be of great political, as well as spiritual, significance; it was the start of a series of major events that changed the course of world history.

In the dream, the Bishop viewed himself reading his morning mail. As he did so, his attention was directed to a large envelope with an ominous black border. Strangely enough, he recognized the handwriting on the envelope to be the forceful script of Archduke Franz Ferdinand, heir apparent to the Austro-Hungarian Empire. Bishop Lanyi was quite certain of the handwriting because the Archduke had been his pupil many years before.

Inside the envelope was a photograph of a crowded street scene. Soldiers lined the road to keep a crowd from the pathway of a luxurious automobile carrying the Archduke, his wife Sophie, an Austrian general, and another army officer.

Suddenly the photograph seemed to come to life, and two men, quite young, rushed from behind the guards and fired revolvers at the Archduke and his wife.

In his dream, the startled Bishop dropped the photograph, then noticed that the Archduke had written a message on its back: "I wish you to know that my wife and I will perish this very day as a result of political assassination. Dear Bishop Lanyi, please say godly prayers and holy Masses for us, and I beseech you to remain devoted to our poor orphaned children."

The letter was dated Sarajevo, June 28, 1914, 3:30 A.M.

The Bishop awakened, disturbed by such a terrible dream. He looked at the clock. It was exactly 3:30 A.M.

Immediately the clergyman went to his desk and wrote down every last detail of the unsettling dream.

After completing this task, he began to say his rosary fervently.

When his butler entered Lanyi's room at 5:30 A.M., he anxiously inquired if the Bishop were ill. Bishop Lanyi told the man that he was extremely upset by a terrible dream in which the holy angels had shown him an awful event that would befall Archduke Franz and Duchess Sophie. He ordered the butler to gather the entire household so that he might say a Mass for the souls of the beloved royal couple.

Bishop Lanyi was a very thorough individual. After the Mass in the chapel had been completed, he told those assembled of his vision and asked that they sign the notes and sketches which he had drawn up from his memory of the dream.

Although there is no record that Bishop Lanyi made any attempt to warn the Crown Prince and his wife of the impending assassination, it is known that the churchman did spend the rest of that day in the chapel, praying continuously for the souls of his country's royalty.

At the same time, several hundred miles away, Archduke Franz Ferdinand and Duchess Sophie were preparing for a day of festivities which would be inaugurated by a lavish parade. Cheering crowds lined the streets of Sarajevo, capital of the province of Bosnia, and the very sight of such warmth and frivolity made the Archduke scoff at the warning that he had received that someone might attempt to assassinate him.

Still, Franz Ferdinand was a Hapsburg and a realist. He was quite aware that if someone among the subjected Serbs did truly seek his life, today's celebration of Vidovdan, their national holiday, would be the perfect time to kill him.

Just before the Crown Prince entered the waiting automobile, he turned to one of his officers and remarked, "It would not surprise me if we were to receive a few bullets today."

The prospect of sudden death did not frighten Franz Ferdinand. He had been instructed from early childhood that he might be required to make his peace with God at the most unexpected moment. The Hapsburg susceptibility to a sudden embrace from the Angel of Death was intensified in Franz Ferdinand's tubercular youth, during which he felt he was living on borrowed time.

The automobile carrying the royal couple did not travel far before it approached the spot where two conspirators stood waiting with hidden revolvers.

The first assassin was nervous and unsteady, for even at point-blank range he missed both of his startled targets.

The second malefactor, the Serbian nationalist Gavrilo Princip, was much steadier and more accurate. His bullets struck first the Archduke, then the Duchess, killing them instantly.

At 3:30 P.M. Bishop Lanyi was interrupted at his prayers to be informed of the deaths of his beloved former pupil Franz Ferdinand and his wife.

SO OFTEN WE HAVE SEEN that the great events of history appear to cast their shadows before them, and so often the angels seem to have had the knowledge to forewarn but not to change the cosmic throw of the dice. The blood of the royal house of Hapsburg had spilled forth from Bishop Lanyi's precognitive dream to become a disastrous reality—and the crimson pool of blood seeping from the violated bodies of Franz Ferdinand and Sophie would flow in ever-widening circles.

On July 28, a month to the day after the Serb Princip had murdered their Crown Prince, Austria declared war on Serbia. Within another week, Germany had declared war on Russia and France, and had invaded Belgium. During that same week, Great Britain declared war on Germany. What the angels had actually shown Bishop Lanyi in that awful vision of assassination was the precipitating event that set the terrible carnage of World War I in motion.

Ireland

AN ANGEL PROVIDED MONEY FOR THE OVERDUE BILL

SIXTY YEARS AGO, MICHAEL DOYLE was born near Ballinasloe, Ireland. He has never forgotten the time that an angel brought his mother the money to pay an overdue bill.

"From her birth, my baby sister Kathleen suffered a chronic illness which the doctors said she would one day outgrow—if we could keep her alive," Michael told us.

"You see, her bronchial tubes would spasm in such away that the poor child could inhale but she couldn't exhale unless someone gave her artificial respiration."

Little Kathleen was in and out of hospitals and clinics, and when she was home the doctor had to visit no less than three times a week.

"I think we were lucky just to scrape by," Michael said. "Although Da made a fairly good living for us, the hospital and doctor bills nearly ate us up. Mother couldn't go back to work, because Kathleen needed constant looking after."

It was in the winter of 1943 that his mother received the money from the angel.

"I was about seven and Kathleen was three or so, and Mother had ordered heavy woolen snowsuits for us to keep away the cold winter winds," Michael continued. "Mother thought that she might be able to squeeze out the money to pay for them by the end of the month of November, but now here it was the middle of March and the bill was long overdue. She knew that if she didn't manage to pay the bill very soon, Da's wages might be garnisheed."

The bill was only a few Irish pounds, around twenty dollars. But, Michael reminded us, in those difficult days of strict rationing in the midst of the strife and stress of World War II, it was a lot of money for a working-class Irish family to set aside for something "extra" like new snowsuits for the kids. He kept expecting his father to grouse about how he and Kathleen could have made do for another winter, but the good man held his peace about the matter.

And then their little miracle occurred.

Mrs. Doyle kept a fern on a stand near the front door, and Michael remembered the day that it suddenly began to shed its leaflets.

"It's looking disgraceful, it is," she worried aloud to Michael. "Help me move it back away from the front door. When the weather is warmer, I'll plant it in the yard for the summer."

Michael recalled that his mother lifted the plant, and he flexed his seven-year-old muscles to manhandle the stand.

"As I did so, the doily that had been under the plant slipped off the stand and an envelope that had been under the doily fell to the floor," Michael remembered. "Strangely enough, it was an airmail envelope, and when Mother opened it, she pulled out crisp, new Irish pound notes—enough to pay her bill at the store and maybe just a wee bit extra."

Michael said that his mother was firmly convinced that God had heard her prayers and had sent an angel to deliver the desperately needed money. It was certain that neither of his parents had put the money under the fern for safekeeping and then forgotten about it. Money was far too scarce in the Doyle household to misplace a single cent, to say nothing of squirreling any of it away.

And they didn't know anyone who could have sent them an airmail letter. Besides, the envelope was unaddressed.

Da and Michael agreed with Mother. The money had come from the angels.

"I always thought the airmail envelope was a very nice touch," Michael said. "After all, the money had come to us through the air from on high."

Italy

ANGELO'S GUARDIAN ANGEL SAVED HIM FROM DROWNING

NGELO DIOTTO OF PADUA, ITALY, has a clear memory of the remarkable event that occurred when he nearly drowned in a swimming pool at the age of ten. He has never forgotten that he was rescued by a heavenly being that identified itself as "Angelo's guardian angel."

Today, as a thirty-eight-year-old adult, Diotto readily admits that he was not a pious little boy. He avoided going to church whenever possible, and his parents grew weary with his constant acts of mischief. The fact that Angelo often behaved like a little devil seemed to make it all the more miraculous that an angel would appear to save him.

The act of angelic intercession took place on July 10, 1968. Angelo had been warned to stay away from the deep end of the swimming pool, but his devil-may-care attitude convinced him that there was nothing to fear if he should decide to jump in. The fact that he didn't yet know how to swim seemed of little consequence.

Angelo decided to jump into the pool at the deep end—and he nearly drowned.

Later, as lifeguards were bringing him around, Angelo said that he had heard beautiful music under the water, and that when he felt the hands of the lifeguards, he did not want them to pull him to the surface.

In fact, after his first few moments of panic, he did not wish to be saved at all.

"I saw things that I had never seen before," Angelo Diotto said. "They were wonderful, beautiful.

"There was a man there who spoke to me and said that he was my guardian angel and that he was always watching over me. He also explained that I often made his task difficult, because I was so mischievous.

"I wanted to run to my guardian angel, but he held both hands up and told me to stay where I was. He said that I should not get too close to him because I was not yet ready to stay where he was. He said that it was unwise, even dangerous, for me to be too near to him, because I must return to the land of the living.

"Then he started to fade away. Everything became a blur, and all of a sudden I was lying on the ground and my mother was crying and men kept pushing some kind of cone over my face."

Ever since that near-death experience as a child, Angelo Diotto said that he has taken great comfort in knowing that there was an entity who called himself "Angelo's guardian angel," who watched over him wherever he went and whatever he did—even though he is no longer quite so mischievous.

Japan

AN ANGEL OPENS THE TELEPHONE LINE

WHILE WE WROTE *ANGELS AROUND THE WORLD*, our youngest daughter, Melissa, was teaching in Japan. Not far from Osaka, she teaches English in Satellite School.

When the giant earthquake hit Japan in 1995, an angel whispered in our ears to turn on the television—there was something we needed to know about immediately! Having learned from experience to trust and obey that voice, we promptly pushed back our chairs, leaving our word processors on as the text cursors flashed away to remind us of the interrupted task at hand.

As soon as the power switch on the television was turned on, it became evident that something of catastrophic proportions had occurred. It took only a few minutes of viewing to find out that an earthquake measuring 7.2 on the Richter scale appeared to have devastated Japan in the Kobe-Osaka region.

Our hearts raced as we ran for the telephone. In dialing the number of Melissa's apartment, it had not even occurred to us to wonder what time it might be in Japan, or when the quake had hit, or whether Melissa would be at home or at the school teaching.

The phone had barely rung when Melissa picked it up, knowing it was us before we spoke. She was okay but extremely shaken—physically and, of course, emotionally. Things had fallen off shelves—dishes, pictures broken, various things in disarray—but thank God the building had not caved in. Nor did it seem that there were buildings down for a couple of blocks or so.

We could talk only long enough to hear she was all right, and the lines went out. We prayed and prayed for her continued protection, as well as for all the people in the area. We did not know at the time we called that the earthquake had occurred many hours before we were finding out about it, and the lines had been down before we called.

Somehow, an angel let us reach our daughter and know that she was safe. From that point on, the lines were down for days, and we could only continue to trust that God and His angels would protect our daughter.

THE DEVASTATION WAS SO GREAT that it was many weeks, months even, before the actual damage and number of those injured or killed could be known. The view of damage from the air was beyond belief. It looked as if the cities had been hit by bombs rather than by an earthquake. Melissa was just a few miles away from Kobe—the area hardest hit.

Shortly afterward, Melissa and a few friends volunteered to help out in feeding the homeless in the heartbreak of their losses. Although the world reached out to send supplies and aid, that didn't stop the ground from shaking with thousands upon thousands of aftershocks, leaving all to wonder if there would be more of the same on the way. Melissa said that a few of the aftershocks were great enough to take down more buildings, which were already "ajar" from the first thunder.

All one can do in such calamities is hope and pray that angels are watching over as many people as possible, guiding them to safety, or keeping their protective wings over such as Melissa. For all those who didn't make it and for all those who lost loved ones, we extend our compassion and sympathy and trust that angels spirited them to a better place in the heavens above.

Mexico

Her Angel Helped Save Her Sons from a Sinking Car

N May 1991, thirty-two-year-old Griselda Dominguez of Zamora, Mexico, was returning home from a brief roadtrip with her two sons, nine-year-old Arturo and seven-year-old Alfredo, when her parked automobile somehow slipped out of gear and rolled into a small lake.

"I was nearly hysterical with fear," she said. "My sons were still in the backseat of the car!"

Griselda had been driving for hours. She stopped the car at the side of the road and got out to stretch her legs for a moment or two and to check the map. Arturo and Alfredo were both sound asleep.

"I know that I turned off the ignition and left the car in 'park.' I was ten or twelve yards from the car when I saw that it was moving. The incline to the lake was quite steep, so once it rolled over the edge, it moved very quickly into the water."

As she made a desperate run to catch up with the runaway car, Griselda screamed at her sons to wake up. "I thought that if they woke up in time, they could somehow get free of the car."

To her absolute horror, once the car rolled into the lake, it began to sink.

Griselda shouted a fervent prayer for assistance. There were no other cars on the road. She was alone with her terrible problem. And she was alone with God and the angels.

"Please, Dear Father," she sobbed, "send one of your ministering angels to help me. I cannot lose my sons!"

Griselda plunged into the lake, swimming furiously to catch up to the sinking automobile.

One back window was open...open enough to squeeze her sons through.

The boys were now wide awake, screaming their terror. The water covered most of the car's body, but it had not yet reached the open window.

"I fought my way through the water," Griselda recalled. "I knew that I couldn't go on living if my sons died. I was so close, I had to save them."

She felt her blood freeze in her veins when the car settled and water suddenly reached the level of the open window. In another few seconds, the car would be completely underwater.

"I could hear my sons screaming to me to save them. I reached the car just as the water began to rush into the open window and engulf my sons."

And then the miracle occurred.

"If I live to be a hundred, I will never forget what I beheld at that moment," Griselda said. "A beautiful being of glowing light appeared under the car and lifted it up so that the rear window was once again above the waterline. My sons were reaching out for me, and I pulled them free of the sinking car.

"Thank God, my husband and I had invested in swimming lessons for the boys. Arturo, especially, swims like a little fish. Once I had them free of the car, I knew that I would be able to guide them toward the shore."

Griselda had no sooner removed Arturo and Alfredo from the open window when the car slipped completely under the water.

"My guardian angel was gone, but he had held the car above water long enough for me to rescue my sons!"

Alfredo became fatigued as they struggled toward land. But a young couple driving by had seen their plight and quickly parked their own car, and the man plunged in to help Griselda bring her boys to safety.

"I have always been a religious person, and I have also known that I had a guardian angel," Griselda said. "And now I know for certain that his strong hand will be there for me whenever I most need it!"

Netherlands

∾

An Angel Saved Him from Drowning— Then Gave Him a Swimming Lesson

ILLY ZANDVOORT TOLD US THAT he had received personalized instruction from a most remarkable swimming coach at his health club in Utrecht, Netherlands.

"In 1991, I was thirty-four years old, and I had still never learned how to swim in an effective style," Willy said. "When I was a little boy, an older cousin taught me how to stay afloat and kick and paddle in the small pond on our farm, but my style was not at all efficient. I would tire easily, and I looked like a harpooned whale threshing and splashing about. I was always embarrassed to have anyone see me in the water, and I avoided swimming parties as a teenager by protesting that I did not know how to swim."

When Willy moved to Utrecht, he joined a health club that had an indoor swimming pool, and he resolved to practice swimming until he had become more proficient in the water.

"But, once again, I was intimidated by the prowess of the other men in the club," he said. "There were expert swimmers who could move through the water as smoothly as eels and who could dive into the pool as confidently as seagulls snatching up fish. I didn't want to be in the way, so I spent most of the time sitting on the side of the pool, just dangling my feet in the water."

Although a sympathetic lifeguard gave him a few tips, Willy remained reluctant to paddle clumsily around the pool and block the paths of more accomplished swimmers.

And then Willy learned that there were few swimmers who used the pool after ten o'clock at night. "Neither was there any lifeguard on duty, but I discovered that I would quite likely have the pool nearly to myself for two hours until the club was locked up at midnight."

Willy enjoyed four or five nights of rigorous practice, and he believed that he was finally beginning to note some improvement in his style. But then came the night when the awful, paralyzing muscle cramp struck him.

"I was all alone in the pool! I had heard of such cramps attacking swimmers, but I had not believed that they could really be so bad, so painful, so debilitating. It seemed as if I could not breathe or move a muscle, and I began to panic. I tried to relax, to stay somehow afloat."

Willy began choking on the water that he was swallowing. He thought that he would be found at midnight, floating facedown, drowned in the pool.

"Seemingly from out of nowhere, I felt strong arms holding me under my armpits. 'Relax,' said a voice in my ear. 'I've got you now. Stay calm. There's nothing to fear.'"

Soon the other swimmer had brought Willy to the shallow end and was kneading the cramped muscles.

"You saved my life," Willy told the man. "I cannot thank you enough. I was in a bad situation there."

Willy remembered his rescuer as a bit over six feet tall, with hair that was whitish-blond, "as if it had been bleached by the sun." The man had a warm smile and a friendly manner and a torso that was well developed, but not especially muscular.

"I will never forget his swimsuit," Willy said. "It was the most distinctive suit that I had ever seen. It was a bright, shiny silver color, as if it were made of polished aluminum or even stainless steel. And it seemed to fit his body like a second skin."

After Willy had rested, his new friend showed him a few moves that greatly improved his swimming stroke.

"He nodded his approval of my improved style, then he seemed almost to rise out of the water in a smooth, fluid movement and began to head toward the door of the pool," Willy said. "I called after him to wait, that I wanted at least to buy him a cup of coffee or tea, but he just waved over his shoulder and walked out the door."

Since the man didn't enter the locker and shower area but left directly by the outer door, Willy assumed that he must be one of the health club employees heading for the front office.

"After I got dressed, I expected to find him sitting in the outer area in a robe with a towel around his wet hair. But when I asked the lone employee still on duty who my friend was, he expressed complete ignorance of such a person— even when I described the distinctive shiny silver swimsuit that he wore."

Glancing at his watch and displaying obvious annoyance at Willy's insistent interrogation, the man impatiently stated that absolutely no one had come out of the pool door except for Willy since a few minutes before ten.

"You've been the only one splashing around in there for the last couple of hours," he told Willy. "It's been a really quiet night. Only a few guys in the weight room. Now can we go home?"

While it may have been a quiet night for the health club attendant, Willy Zandvoort concluded, "I know that my guardian angel saved me from drowning—and taught me a few swimming tips at the same time. It was far from a quiet night for me!"

Norway

BROUGHT BACK FROM DEATH BY HER ANGEL— AND HER HUSBAND'S LOVE

N 1987, KRISTA TJADEN, who lives in a small town outside of Oslo, wrote to tell us about the awful night nearly fifteen years earlier when she died in her sleep. According to her understanding, it was only the intervention of her guardian angel and the love of her husband Jon that prevented her from passing to the other side.

Krista awakened one night in February, 1972, with a terrible pain that seemed to move from her abdominal region to her heart. "The pain was unbearable," she said, when she and Jon talked with us later. "I had a fleeting thought that I must be dying...and then I passed out."

At the same time, Jon lay dreaming that Krista had been shot by a thief as she walked on the street of a mountain village. "Police officers came running up, and they, in turn, shot the thug, but all that was too late to do Krista any good," he said. "In this awful dream, I saw them stretch Krista's body out on a park bench, and I ran to her and knelt by her side. With tears streaming down my cheeks, I kept shouting, 'Don't leave me! Oh, dear Krista, please don't leave me!'"

Krista said that in her reality she suddenly found herself walking through unfamiliar hilly and barren country.

"All around me was dark and dreary. I heard Jon shouting from somewhere in the darkness, 'Krista, please don't leave me.' His words kept repeating over and over again. I wanted to move, yet I could not. I wanted to answer him, but no sound came from my throat. I no longer had any control over my body."

It was at that frightening moment that Krista beheld a glowing figure of light manifesting before her. "I seemed to be able to make out these two beautiful blue eyes filled with pure love looking out at me from the bright light, but I could distinguish no other features. The brilliant light was in the shape of a human, but I can only describe the angel as being somehow composed of pure light."

Krista recalled that she seemed to hear a message from the angel that reverberated inside her very essence. "The angel said that it was not yet my time to cross to the other side. He said that Jon and I had things to learn together— and that I was to bear two children who would have a special mission to perform on Earth."

Dimly, Krista became aware of Jon sitting up in bed and turning her over on her back. "I felt just a trickle of life returning to my body. I found myself awake, My sleeping husband bending over me.

"Although Jon had turned me over and rubbed my neck, chest, and hands, he never once fully awakened despite his exertions. I lay there for quite some time, cautiously testing all my major body parts to see if everything was working again. At last I drifted into an uneasy sleep."

Jon, however, was still locked in his terrible nightmare about seeing his beloved Krista shot down by a hoodlum. "Krista was no longer lying still and cold on the park bench where the police officers had placed her," Jon said. "I saw her walking away from me into a strange and barren land. I tried to follow her, but I could not get past an invisible barrier. *I knew that she would leave me forever unless I could get her back.*"

Although Jon could not enter the dark, barren terrain, he could stand at the border and call to Krista to return. "I cried over and over again, 'My darling Krista, please don't leave me. Come back to me!'

"And suddenly this brilliant ball of light was leading her to me. 'Take her quickly,' a voice said from within the light. 'Take her by the hand and pull her back to life.'"

The next thing Jon knew, he was bending over Krista in their bed, refusing to accept her death.

"I knew that I was in some kind of trancelike state when this beautiful angel appeared beside us and told me that I had been given a gift of healing from the heavenly host. The angel told me to turn Krista over on her back and to keep massaging her and to keep projecting thoughts of love to her."

When the alarm went off that morning, Krista awakened to find Jon holding her close to him.

"Jon told me about his dream and how the angel had told him to keep massaging me and sending me thoughts of love," she said. "We lay there for several minutes marveling over the strange manner in which dream states may be shared."

Finally Jon raised himself on an elbow and started to speak—then stopped, a ghastly pallor draining his features of their normal ruddiness. He reached over to the bedside table and handed Krista a mirror.

"One look shocked me," Krista said. "The skin under my eyes, around my mouth, and at the edges of my nostrils was blue. My flesh was cold and lifeless to the touch. My fingernails were blue, and so were my toenails and the palms of my hands. My whole body was rather unmanageable. Also, Jon noticed a place in my right eye where the white seemed to have congealed. Gradually, the bluish color left my fingernails and my palms, and I regained the use of my body after a few hours—but it took a week for all the blue on my face to go away. And I still have the spot in my eye after all this time.

"Once when a medical doctor saw the spot in my eye, he said that I must have come very close to death at some time for such a spot to have formed."

Krista and Jon went on to have two children, who at the time they contacted us were thirteen and eleven years old.

"Both Loren and Karla are very serious-minded children who are already considering pursuing studies in social work or education," Jon said. "We know that they will soon be fulfilling the prophecy that Krista's angel made about their doing 'special work' here on Earth."

A prophecy, Krista added, that nearly cost their mother her life.

The Philippines

HER GUARDIAN ANGEL JOINED HER FOR LUNCH

OME YEARS AGO, A MISSIONARY FRIEND named Mary told us that any doubts that she might have had about angels working directly in the lives of humans were immediately put to rest when she experienced her own angelic encounter.

It happened while she was in the Philippine Islands on mission work, during her very first visit to a private home. Perhaps the initial clue that her unseen guardian was at hand was provided when her hostess expressed surprise that the house's two giant guard dogs had not barked to announce the arrival of a stranger.

In the dining room, Mary was perplexed when her hostess proceeded to pull out two chairs—both, apparently, for Mary. Chuckling to herself, Mary reflected that she knew she had gained a few pounds, but certainly not enough to warrant two chairs.

Once Mary was seated, she smiled, observed the amenities, then noticed her gracious hostess setting another place at the table.

"It dawned on me that the other chair was quite likely for a family member or another guest who had not yet arrived," Mary said. "I was tempted to inquire who else was expected for lunch, but since I was not quite certain of Philippine customs, I thought it best not to."

Finally the hostess sat down and motioned for Mary to begin eating her lunch. Mary hesitated. The other chair remained empty. Wasn't it rude to begin eating when another guest was expected? However, when it was quite clear that the hostess was not at all reluctant to begin, Mary picked up her utensils and began.

After a few moments, their "getting to know you" conversation flowed easily. Mary found that she was enjoying herself and the wonderful company, yet she was very curious about why the hostess often looked at the empty chair throughout their lunch. At times, the hostess even appeared to be talking and gesturing to the chair as if it held an actual person.

"I'm afraid that I was just about convinced that my charming hostess might not be quite 'all there,' when I noticed that the full glass of milk that had been placed in front of the empty chair was almost empty," Mary said. "I know that my mouth must have dropped open, for there had been no one there to drink it."

Mary finally resolved to put thoughts of the empty chair and the disappearing milk out of her mind. The visit was otherwise going well.

A few more hours passed quickly, and Mary suddenly became concerned about overstaying her welcome.

As good-byes were being said at the door, Mary was again perplexed by her hostess when she put one arm around Mary's shoulders and the other around thin air.

"How nice it was, Mary, that your friend came with you," the courteous woman smiled.

Mary was stunned, and felt her knees buckle.

"Then it all became very clear to me," she told us. "Before I had started out for the woman's house, I had prayed extra hard for protection because I had heard that she lived in a rough neighborhood. I glanced back at the chair at the table and the nearly empty glass of milk at the place setting, and I thanked God for this extraordinary evidence that my prayer had been answered. I had been truly blessed to have had an angel companion who joined me for lunch."

Turkey

"You Are Your Brother's Keeper"

USTAFA OZAL, WHO NOW RESIDES in Boston, told us of the angelic encounter that he experienced as a young man in Ankara, Turkey.

"My father had been killed in an automobile accident in 1947," he said. "When Mother became ill in 1951, my older sister was already married, but my younger brother Suleiman and I lived at home. Mother's condition steadily worsened, and she knew that she would soon be joining our father in paradise.

"One night, just a few days before she died, Mother called me to her bedside and asked me to take a vow that I would look after Suleiman. I had just turned twenty. I had a good job and was taking some university courses. Suleiman was seventeen, quite lazy, and inclined to run with a wild crowd of young men."

Mustafa said that because of his great love for his mother he made a promise to keep an eye on Suleiman. "But I knew that I would have my hands full looking after the rascal, and I somewhat resented having such responsibility placed on my head."

Two months after their mother had passed away, Suleiman had established a regular routine of late hours carousing with his companions. He soon lost his part-time job, and he began to neglect his studies at the trade school. Mustafa urged his brother to change his reckless ways and take life more seriously, but he made no real effort to curb Suleiman's destructive lifestyle.

"I had more or less turned my back on Suleiman and concentrated more on ignoring him than on attempting to alter his worthless ways," Mustafa admitted. "My dream was to go to America and become a citizen of the United States. I did not wish Suleiman's bad habits to block my plans for advancement."

One night at about midnight, Mustafa was awakened by the sound of someone calling his name. "I rolled over in bed, and I was astonished to behold a magnificent angelic being in a long, flowing white robe standing beside me. The angel seemed to be glowing so brightly that I had to shield my eyes."

And then, in a very clear and authoritative voice, the being told Mustafa that Suleiman was in great danger.

"You made a promise to your mother," the angel reminded him. "You vowed that you would take care of your brother. Know this, Mustafa, you are your brother's keeper! You must go at once to the place where you know he gambles and bring him home. He is in very great danger."

Having delivered the warning, the majestic being disappeared and left Mustafa trembling in awe and fear. "I knew that I could not disregard such an admonition, so I got dressed and prepared to set out at once for the den of ill repute where I knew Suleiman and his boisterous crowd hung out.

"At first Suleiman was angry and defiant when I walked into the place," he recalled. "His rowdy bunch of friends hooted at me and shouted insults, but I managed to draw Suleiman apart from them so that we could talk privately. Strangely enough, he became very quiet and attentive when I told him about the remarkable angelic visitation that I had experienced. And when I stressed that the angel had said that he was in great danger, Suleiman agreed to leave with me."

The next day at work, Mustafa learned that a quarrel had escalated to a knife fight among the gamblers at the den frequented by Suleiman.

"Two of Suleiman's friends had been badly injured, and another had been killed," Mustafa said. "If the angelic being had not reminded me of my responsibility to my brother and my promise to my mother, he might have been a casualty or a fatality of the fight. Suleiman experienced a dramatic change in his lifestyle that day, and in five years we were both able to come to America to establish new lives."

The United States

California

 WICE IN HIS LIFE, A. R. THOMPSON has been saved by the voice of an angelic guide, and he is convinced that there are benevolent beings that guide our lives—if we will but listen.

Thompson first became aware of his guardian angel's presence in 1947 when he was being discharged from the army and processed home from the occupation forces in Japan. He was offered his choice of traveling by ship or airplane, and since he had been separated from his family in the States for so long, he unhesitatingly chose to travel by plane.

Six hours before he was scheduled to depart from the Tokyo airport, he lay on his bunk and thought lovingly of the family that he had not seen for two years.

"It would be wiser to go home by ship," a voice from out of nowhere suddenly told him.

Thompson jumped out of his bunk and looked around him. The barracks was empty—yet the voice sounded as though it had been speaking directly into his ear.

Assured that he was alone, he lay back down on his bunk.

The voice spoke again, sounding so clear and natural that Thompson would have sworn there was someone standing next to him. *"You should go home by ship."*

Thompson had heard of people who claimed to hear voices from other spheres, but he had always dismissed such stories as delusions or exaggerations. He sat for a few moments on the edge of his bunk, attempting to steady his nerves. And then the eerie thought struck him: What if this was a genuine mystical experience and he was truly receiving heavenly advice from an angel? Should he heed the unseen speaker?

He lay back on his bunk, trying his best to convince himself that he was just overtired.

"Please believe me! It will be better for you if you go home by ship."

That did it! Thompson figured that three times was enough for the hardiest of skeptics.

He went straight to his commanding officer and informed him that he had changed his mind. He wished to return by ship.

"All right," the. officer scowled. "I'll try."

As it turned out, there was a great deal of resistance to Thompson's sudden and unexpected requests and several times he felt like forgetting the bother. Each time, though, something checked him, and he stood firm in his resolve.

Finally the change in travel plans was confirmed, and Thompson's commanding officer booked him aboard a homeward-bound ship scheduled to leave Tokyo the next week.

Three hours later the plane on which Thompson had been scheduled to leave for the States crashed during takeoff, killing all on board.

Thompson was terribly shaken by the grim news and gave thanks for the strange warning process that had managed to keep him off the plane.

A COUPLE OF YEARS LATER, while visiting his mother in Los Angeles, Thompson was invited to a friend's home for dinner. Little did he know when he accepted the invitation to meet the man's family and wax nostalgic about college days that he would be inviting his guardian angel to manifest once again.

To get to his friend's home in the San Fernando Valley, Thompson had to go by way of Cahuenga Pass, a busy speedway that was nearly always clogged with traffic on weekends. Anticipating difficulties and delays, he allowed himself a full hour for travel.

True to his concern, he soon found cars lined up bumper to bumper, and he became excruciatingly aware of the minutes ticking away. When he could finally pull away from the slow-moving mass of automobiles, he pushed hard on the accelerator.

He had gone no more than a mile when he distinctly heard a voice speaking in his ear: *"You had better stop the car."*

Thompson gave a start. The instant that he heard the voice his mind was filled with memories of the tragic plane crash at the Tokyo airport. Even so, he resisted the command to stop the car in the middle of one of the busiest freeways in Los Angeles.

"You had better stop the car immediately!"

Thompson thought once more of the horrible plane crash, and he began to slow down.

A stream of angrily honking cars roared past him as he drew off to the side of the road and stopped his automobile.

"All right," he wondered aloud. "What am I to do now?"

"Get a tow truck. Do not drive this car any farther."

Thompson decided that he might as well obey his invisible advisor. He turned off the car—the car that seemed to be running just fine—and walked to a pay phone. He found the number of a garage in the area and requested a tow truck.

Later, when the mechanic with the truck asked him what was wrong with the car, Thompson said that he had no idea.

Frowning his impatience, the mechanic checked under the hood. "Looks and sounds great to me, pal," he said after a few moments' inspection.

"Well, I'm *not* driving it," Thompson said resolutely.

The mechanic gave him another frown. "It's your money."

After the mechanic hitched the bumper to the hoist and lifted the front of the car off the ground, Thompson got into the cab of the truck.

The tow truck had moved no more than five feet when the two men heard a loud crash behind them. The mechanic slammed on the brakes and they jumped out of the cab.

There, on the pavement, lay the front wheel of Thompson's car. It had simply fallen off the axle.

Without saying another word, the mechanic picked up the wheel and put it in the back of the truck. The two men drove in silence back to the garage.

THE DINNER THAT HIS FRIEND'S WIFE had prepared was quite cold by the time Thompson arrived. He could only offer the excuse of car trouble. He made no effort to tell the couple about the angelic guardian who had once again saved his life.

But he knew that if he had not obeyed his angel's voice, he would most assuredly have had an accident. Not only might he have been killed, but he would undoubtedly have brought injury and perhaps even death to others on the busy freeway.

In the May 1955 issue of *Fate* magazine, Thompson expressed his gratitude to the unseen guardian who had saved his life on two separate occasions. And he added: "I advise anyone who may be visited by…another of his kind to heed his voice. Do not hesitate to obey his command, no matter how incomprehensible it may seem. You may not be given another chance."

Missouri

∾

ANGELS GAVE HIM THE STRENGTH TO TRIUMPH
OVER CHILDHOOD ABUSE

HOWARD GUTHRIE TOLD US that angels came to him when he was a child in rural Missouri and gave him the love and support necessary to withstand terrible abuse.

He remembered that he was about five years old when—for some reason he was never able to determine—he became the official physical scapegoat for the other members of his family. Whenever anything in their lives went wrong, Howard was beaten in an almost ritualistic manner by both of his parents and his two older brothers.

One night, when he was about eleven, his father whipped him into unconsciousness for no special reason and left him lying on the ground in back of the corncrib.

"When I awoke, it was dark and I was looking up at the stars," Howard said. "Since we lived out in the country and we didn't have any yard light to mask out the stars, it was like I could see straight up into Heaven. I started to cry, because I really wanted to go home to Heaven that night. I was in a lot of pain because Pa had whipped me so hard. I was lying on the soft, cool grass, and I knew that if I went into the house and up into the room I shared with my brothers, they would probably beat up on me and make me sleep on the floor.

So I just lay there, and I started to pray for God to send some angels to come and take me away."

In his childish reasoning, Howard believed that if he just willed himself not to wake up in the morning, he would be dead and God would have to send angels to claim his soul.

"I started noticing seven unusually bright stars moving around the sky, and then I saw that they were coming closer and closer to me. They stopped about twenty feet above the apple orchard, then they slowly lowered themselves to the ground and began coming toward me."

Howard insisted that he was not afraid. "I just thought that a merciful God had granted my prayer and sent his angels to bring me home to Heaven."

The seven glowing, pulsating beings formed a circle around Howard as he lay on the grass in the farmyard. They seemed to float, rather than walk, and he could see their beautiful robes moving ever so slightly as they hovered around him and began to sway in a side-to-side motion.

"I heard a strange kind of musical humming sound, as if the angels were singing. And then I noticed that the pain from the whipping was leaving me."

After the physical healing had taken place, the angelic beings started "putting images" in Howard's mind. "It was kind of like they were showing me a really positive, upbeat movie inside my head. I can't remember everything I saw. I just recall that it was all really inspirational and joyful. I started feeling a tingling sensation, and then, I guess, I fell asleep."

When he awakened the next morning, Howard was suffused with a marvelous sense of purpose for his life. He knew that he would withstand the family's cruelty toward him and rise above the demeaning and debilitating effects of their abuse.

Howard said that he received occasional angelic visitations and "mental movies" all through his adolescent years and up until the time he entered military service.

Although his family was unchurched and did not possess a Bible, nearly all of his visions were of a spiritual or religious nature.

"Once I had entered military service, I was totally free of my family," Howard told us. "When I was discharged, I entered college and got a degree in education. I've been a teacher now for twelve years. I'm happily married, with two children. I owe my life and my sanity to those angels who formed that circle around my whipped and battered physical vehicle and healed both my body and my soul on that long-ago night of torment."

New Jersey

THE ANGELS HAVE ALWAYS LOOKED AFTER DEBORA

ANET DEAN OF WENONAH, NEW JERSEY, is certain that her daughter Debora is a special child who is beloved of the angels.

Consider this incredible episode she presents as only one example:

On a late-winter afternoon in 1993, two-year-old Debora ran ahead of Janet as they entered a second-floor bedroom. The exuberant child ran across the room, jumped up on a chair in front of an open window—and fell out.

Janet's absolute and total horror was immediately transformed into amazement when she beheld her little girl being transported *backwards* into the room.

Later, after her nerves had calmed down to some degree, Janet reflected that the experience was like seeing a motion picture film projected in reverse. She could remember screaming for help—and then, just as quickly as little Debora had fallen out of the window, she came flying back in.

None the worse for what could have been a fatal fall, Debora stood in front of Janet and greeted her with a cheery, "Hi, Mommy," just as if nothing unusual had occurred.

"There is no doubt about it," Janet said. "It was Debora's guardian angel who caught her and carried her back inside. I picked her up in my arms and cried with relief."

Janet believes that angels have always looked after her daughter. "Once, Debora put her foot through a glass door. It shattered, but there wasn't a single cut on her."

New Mexico

God Sent an Angel with Muscles to Lift a Car Off a Teenage Boy

N August 1987, seventeen-year-old Ray Santos of Las Cruces, New Mexico, was repairing the transmission of his 1978 Chevrolet in the backyard of his home when the car slipped off the rack and pinned him.

A steel cross-brace under the steering column pressed heavily and agonizingly against his chest. The pain was unbearable. He felt as though the very life was being crushed out of him.

He tried to take a deep breath, but he couldn't. And every time he shouted for help, he let air out of his lungs—and the terrible weight on his chest increased.

The last thing that Ray remembered before he blacked out was asking God to forgive his sins.

The Santos's next-door neighbor, sixty-six-year-old Felicita Madrid, heard the boy's faint cries for help as she worked in her kitchen. When she looked out of her window and saw a pair of shoes sticking out from under the Chevrolet, she knew that someone was being killed. Her shouts brought Ray's mother

Estelle; another neighbor, Roberta Gavarette; and Roberta's eleven-year-old daughter, Rita.

Estelle Santos cried out in an anguished prayer for God the Father to send a miracle. "Please help us lift the car off Ray before he dies!"

And then, realizing that they had no time to waste watching the heavens for a sign of comfort, the two women and the girl began trying their best to lift a three-thousand-pound automobile off the unconscious teenage boy being crushed to death by its relentless bulk.

It was when they were about to try again at the count of three that the stranger ran up to them.

"He was not an especially tall man," Estelle Santos recalled later. "But he was stocky and powerfully built. There was something about him that was kind of strange, fierce, and wild—but his brown eyes were kind."

The stranger wedged himself between the women. "Let me give you a hand!"

Estelle Santos counted to three again. "And when we lifted the bumper, the big man's muscles bulged—and the car rose completely off the ground. It now seemed as light as a feather."

The powerful stranger told Felicita and Rita to pull Ray out from under the car while he and the other two women held the car off his chest.

In the next few minutes of excitement, the ambulance arrived to take Ray to the hospital, and the stranger with all the muscles disappeared.

The teenager was very lucky and, miraculously, suffered no broken bones or internal injuries. He was thankful to be alive, but was upset that his mother hadn't gotten the stranger's name so that they could thank him properly.

"The important thing is that God heard our prayers and spared my son's life," she said. "He granted us a miracle by sending us a powerful helping hand."

~ *Epilogue* ~

For to his angels he has given command about you,
that they guard you in all your ways.
—PSALM 91:11

Every man hath a good and a bad angel attending on him in particular,
all his life long.
—ROBERT BURTON

IT IS OUR TRUE BELIEF that all things work together for good for those who love God. However, we have been given free will—and that is the problem. The great difficulty in all of our lives on Earth is acquiring the discernment to tell the difference between the good and the bad.

We have seen in our research and in our counseling how many individuals believe they have heard "the voice of God" or "the voice of an angel" tell them to do things that turned out to be clearly wrong.

We must always bear in mind that there are good angels and bad (fallen) angels. So just because we believe that an angel has given us a particular bit of advice, it does not necessarily mean that it is the right thing to do. The Bible reminds us always to "test and try" the spirits and the angels. We must know at all times with whom we are dealing!

There are millions upon millions of angels with different assignments, capacities, and missions. There are guardian angels, warrior angels, angels of love and light, healing angels, angels of joy, angel record keepers, and so on. We are also told that there are many levels of angels, from those that are just "a little higher" than we, to those angelic beings that surround God and are with him at his heavenly throne.

One of the reasons why the priests and various church fathers may have kept the records of angelic acts away from the masses for such a long time may have been precisely the same as our reason for strongly advising certain cautions now—and that is to avoid "angelolatry," a worship of the angels.

Remember that we humans are just a little lower than the angels. This, according to all holy teachings, means that there may be countless angelic beings with not a great deal more discernment than we have as finite creatures on Earth. While they may indeed have a heavenly purpose and a godly mission, that does not mean that we should ever worship or pray to them—just as we should not pray to a wise or highly spiritual fellow human.

Rather, it is given to us to pray to the one Living God and then trust that our prayer will set in motion the mission of the angels. It is to that end and purpose that we celebrate and honor the beauty of God's holy design together with the care and protection of his couriers, his messengers, the angels.

⌇ A NOTE FROM THE EDITORS ⌇

This book was selected by the book division of the company that publishes *Guideposts*, a monthly magazine filled with true stories of people's adventures in faith, and *Angels on Earth*, a bimonthly magazine that presents true stories about God's angels and humans who have played angelic roles in daily life.

Guideposts magazine and *Angels on Earth* are not sold on the newsstand. They are available by subscription only. And subscribing is easy. All you have to do is write to Guideposts, 39 Seminary Hill Road, Carmel, New York 10512.

When you subscribe, you can count on receiving exciting new evidence of God's presence, His guidance and His limitless love for all of us.

Guideposts is also available on the Internet by accessing our homepage on the World Wide Web at http://www.guideposts.org. Send prayer requests to our Monday morning Prayer Fellowship. Read stories from recent issues of our magazines, *Guideposts*, *Angels on Earth*, *Guideposts for Kids* and *Positive Living*, and follow our popular book of daily devotionals, *Daily Guideposts*. Excerpts from some of our best-selling books are also available.